CW00662113

VICTORIAN VILLAGE LIFE

VICTORIAN
VILLAGE
LIFE

NEIL PHILIP

With a Preface by
Gordon Mingay
Emeritus Professor of Agrarian History, University of Kent

ALBION

For John Philip

An Albion Book

First published in Great Britain in 1993 by
The Albion Press Ltd,
Spring Hill,
Idbury,
Oxfordshire, OX7 6RU

Distributed by Melia Publishing Services
P.O. Box 1639, Maidenhead, Berks SL6 6YZ

Designer: Emma Bradford
Project Manager: Elizabeth Wilkes

Copyright © Neil Philip 1993
Preface copyright © G. E. Mingay 1993
The wood-engravings by Myles Birket Foster are reproduced from
Pictures of English Landscape (1863)

All rights reserved. No part of this publication may be reproduced, stored in a
retrieval system, or transmitted, in any form or by any means, electronic,
mechanical, photocopying, recording or otherwise, without the prior written
permission of the copyright holders. The moral rights of the author have been
asserted.

ISBN 1 871927 05 6

Typesetting by York House Typographic, London
Printed and bound in Great Britain by The Bath Press

CONTENTS

IN TIME OF "THE BREAKING OF NATIONS"

I

Only a man harrowing clods
  In a slow silent walk
With an old horse that stumbles and nods
  Half asleep as they stalk.

II

Only thin smoke without flame
  From the heaps of couch-grass;
Yet this will go onward the same
  Though Dynasties pass.

III

Yonder a maid and her wight
  Come whispering by
War's annals will cloud into night
  Ere their story die.

THOMAS HARDY

PREFACE

WHAT WAS IT like to live in a Victorian village? Neil Philip's account
of the old rural society vividly evokes the essence of a now long-lost
countryside. It seems worthwhile to preface his account of village life
with a survey of the forces which shaped it. His villagers, it has to be
remembered, lived and worked within an economic and social framework that was radically different from the highly market-oriented,
regulated, subsidized structure that permeates agriculture and the
relationships between farmer and farmworker today.

In the Victorian era the landed estate still dominated much the
greater area of the countryside and influenced not only agriculture
itself but also the lives of the estate's inhabitants: the landowner's
employees directly, the tenant farmer and his work people at one
remove. Today the major part of the farmland is owned by the people
who farm it, but the Victorian owner-occupier was in a distinct
minority, owning under a fifth of the total. Although towards the end
of the nineteenth century depression conditions obliged many landowners to take land over from failing tenants and farm it themselves,
in previous times the proprietors of estates rarely farmed for profit,
though they might keep a home farm near the mansion for the
convenience of having fresh supplies on the doorstep or to satisfy an
interest in trying out pedigree stock or progressive techniques.

Their farms, varying in size according to the nature of the farming,
were let to tenant farmers. In some districts these were men of large
capital, farming extensive acreages and employing a labour force that
ran to fifty or seventy strong, and holding the land on the terms fixed
by a legally binding lease; or they might more often be small family
farmers, working on a modest scale and employing few hands
beyond those of their own wife, sons and daughters. They rarely had
the security of a lease but went on from year to year confident in the
unwritten understanding that the landlord would not displace them

9

so long as they farmed reasonably well, were not too backward in paying their rent, and were not so fond of carousing or fornicating as to bring the estate into disrepute. In this manner a family sometimes held the same farm over several generations, passing it on from father to son, even to widow or daughter.

To the casual observer the estate-dominated countryside might seem unchanging. Gatherings at country houses still influenced government, and even at the end of the century the representatives of great landed families still bulked large in government. But, as so often, appearances were misleading, concealing an impending decline of landed power just as agriculture itself had declined from pre-eminence to the position of only one among a number of large industries. Moreover, the political interests of town-dwellers – in a growing majority since mid-century – came to predominate over those of the country. This was seen most evidently in the two extensions of the franchise to incorporate lower social strata, and elimination of the former interference by owners and their agents at the polls. As a consequence, when from the 1870s onwards the 1846 Repeal of the Corn Laws really began to hurt landowners and farmers, the question of an early return to effective protection was politically not on the cards.

The agricultural depression heralded the onset of a new climate of increasingly effective international competition, falling grain prices, and pressure on landlords faced with the choice of reducing rents or being obliged to take farms into hand. Land still conferred social status, but it no longer provided the means for maintaining it. While landlords economized, sold outlying properties, let out their shooting, and even abandoned the mansion itself, their tenants – often newcomers to the estate – struggled on, helped by lower rents, the continued expansion of urban markets, and by shifting into lines of production in which there was less or no foreign competition, into milk, hay, and fruit and vegetables. They cut back on inessential work around the farm, reduced their labour force, and frequently combined farming with some other business. Increasingly the farmers came to realise that the old reliance on the landowner to take up their grievances and bring pressure to bear in high places was no longer a solution to hard times. Their loyalty declined, little by little, as new country organizations, still headed by landowners, proved impotent to mend matters, and early in the new century the farmers broke away completely to form the National Farmers' Union, from which landowners and their agents were pointedly excluded.

How, in all this, fared the workfolk, as the farmworkers often referred to themselves? Their own attempts in the 1870s to form a powerful national union foundered on the rocks of farmer hostility, lock-outs and evictions from their homes, the onset of the depression, and not least dissensions within the union itself. Nevertheless, their conditions did slowly improve, aided primarily by a gradual reduction in their numbers as many moved off the land or emigrated; while those remaining on the land were helped especially by the fall in the prices of food and other necessities which marked the closing decades of Victoria's reign. Their wages advanced only slowly in money terms, but money was now going further, and by the end of the century there is clear evidence of better living standards in terms of a more varied diet and the possession of petty luxuries such as watches and bicycles. A growing scarcity of good hands led to farmers pursuing men, rather than the other way round; newly-established Board schools provided some country children with the possibility of improving themselves; and the womenfolk were less frequently seen labouring in the fields. This is not to say that there was not still a large measure of deprivation and suffering. Working hours remained very long and holidays very few, adults and children were frequently under-nourished, and housing, while slowly improved, remained very patchy, with a scarcity of good cottages and too many consisting of old converted farm buildings and insanitary two-room hovels. At the end of the road – and many farmworkers lived as long as did their employers, that is to say, considerably longer than most town-dwellers – there loomed only the bleak unwelcome shelter of the workhouse.

The culture of the workfolk was changing too. Hardy and others deplored the decline of the old songs, customs, and legends. Belief in folk remedies was declining, and resort to magic – the advice of a 'cunning man' or a 'wise woman', for instance – was gradually dying out, the traditional observances required at deaths, births and marriages coming to be remembered only by the elderly. Exposure to the culture of the towns, to schooling, to the popular newspaper, hastened on these changes.

The innovation of oral history, as practised for example by George Ewart Evans, came only just in time to preserve elements of the traditional lore. But the historian who troubles to search for the ideas and feelings expressed in now forgotten old poems, songs, and out-of-the-way reminiscences, can do much to reconstruct the traditional culture which has receded beyond the reach of the tape recorder, and as in this volume, create a sense of what it was really like to live among the villagers of the last century, to share their times of joy and suffering, and the unending toil of earning the daily bread.

Gordon Mingay

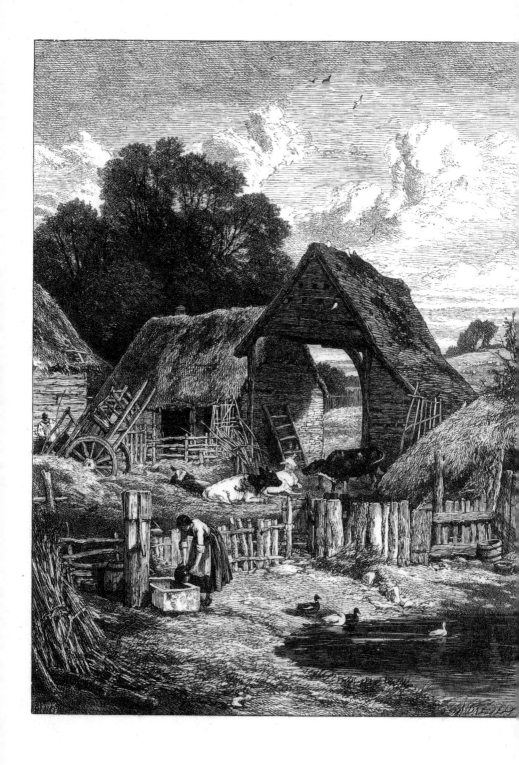

INTRODUCTION

TO MODERN EYES, conditioned by the exquisite watercolours of Helen Allingham or Birket Foster, and by the romantic recreations of period films, the Victorian village looks an idyllic place. No cars, no ferti- lisers, none of the stresses and strains of modern life: all is picturesque and charming.

Indeed the Victorian urban and suburban middle classes cherished as we do what Graham Robertson called Helen Allingham's 'lovely little transcripts' of country life. The pleasantly prettified village sketches of Mary Russell Mitford were never out of print, and the Victorians responded as warmly as we do to her 'busy, merry, stirring little world'.

One of the more hard-headed of all the social explorers who recorded the Victorian countryside, G.F. Millin, has left one of the most evocative pictures of this idyll-that-never-was, in his descrip- tion of a village in Suffolk bordering on Norfolk:

> Here is a vicarage garden with a party at lawn tennis; yonder through that woody vista is a little company of harvesters; now you have a rosy-looking woman shaking down the plums for a fair-haired child, and further on you see a venerable-looking dame sitting by the open door amid flowers and beehives. Peace and quiet, beauty and fruitful- ness, prevail everywhere. The village shoemaker is deliberately stitch- ing away in a breezy little workshop, with the scarlet blossoms of kidney beans glowing in at the open door, and hollyhocks and rosy apples peering in at the window, out of which the good man now and again gazes as though in heart he is out with the reapers yonder in the waving cornfield. We push our way through the stalwart, standing corn down towards a cottage clad in grapevine and half-buried in the brown rustling wheat, where stands the village blacksmith, not under a spreading chestnut-tree but, better still, within the shadow of a well- laden pear-tree, planted knee-deep in the corn on the margin of his own

cornfield. Sickle in hand, and with two or three young men about him, the burly smith, with his cornsheaves and his pear-tree and the cosy cottage just over the hedge there all combine to make a picture such as, one cannot but think, must often haunt the memory of the emigrants from rural England into the docks and railway depots and warehouses of London.

The longing of the sophisticated for a simple life, and of the urbanised for a rural one, had already taken hold. Against such a strong mental image of peace, contentment, healthy hard work and honest fare, no evidence to a Royal Commission about the real conditions of the countryside could make much headway. Writers then as now tried to use the strength of this romantic appeal against itself, entitling a powerful series of investigative reports into village living conditions *The 'Romance' of Peasant Life*, or a disenchanted record of life in a poor rural parish *Arcady, for Better, for Worse*.

For the truth was that the English countryside in the last half of the nineteenth century, for all its seductive beauty, was falling apart. The conditions Richard Heath found in Sussex in 1871 could be paralleled across the country:

In Rotherfield I went into one cottage where a woman sat in the grimy chimney corner, trying to make a kettle boil over a few sticks of wood. Two little girls were hanging over the dying embers, for it was miserably cold. The mother took us upstairs, where there were two compartments. In the first, a sort of landing, the parents slept on a miserable bed almost on a level with the floor. In a small outer room was a little shake-down on which the children slept. Not a chair, not a table, nor any other article of furniture, was in the room. In the parents' sleeping place the wet came in, so that the woman said one night she was wet through. She had had ten children, but had only reared two. One boy died when he was nine; the others slowly died mostly of decline and galloping consumption – slow starvation, in fact! For this miserable habitation they paid two shillings a week. It had, however, a garden, in which they raised cabbages. Her husband earned, on an average, ten shillings a week all the year round.

Of course most rural parishes contained a mixed society, often with a strong middle or upper working class element. As Richard Jefferies put it, 'A rural parish, if a well-selected specimen, forms of itself a miniature state, and contains representatives of the chief varieties of human life.' But the vast majority of the rural population were labourers and their families, and it was on this section of society that the changing conditions of the Victorian era bore down hardest. In her marvellous history of the Gloucestershire village of Bledington, *The Changing English Village*, M.K. Ashby points out that it is no mistake that 'The poor used the same word for suffering from lack of food and from cold – "starvation".'

The English rural poor were not a peasantry. They had no stake in the land, and their overlords had little sense of feudal responsibility towards them. A farmer might hire a man for the summer and turn him into the workhouse for the winter, with as little thought as someone today putting their lawnmower away for the season.

This account of life in the English village concentrates on the poor, on the employed rather than on the employers. In many ways, while the face which the village turned to the outside world was that of its squire, parson and farmers, the true heart of village life lay in the unofficial, largely unrecorded world of the cottager. Increasingly in the nineteenth century, farmers and landowners lived outside and apart from the village, and, for all the power they wielded, they were largely irrelevant to the daily concerns of the villagers. As Lady Eleanor Acland, whose family owned a paper-mill in Westmorland, recalled:

> We knew very little of the people in our village, most of whom worked in the family business. . . . The nearest we came to having any natural fun with the village children was at the annual 'Gala' when we were allowed to join in the juvenile races, and had to win or lose on our merits.

In the chapters which follow, I hope to bring the vanished world of the Victorian village to life: at work, at leisure, and in the process of change. Inevitably, what is true for one village or area may not be for another. As Augustus Jessopp wrote, 'The truth is that no two country parishes in England are so alike in their social, moral and physical conditions as to admit of their being treated in precisely the same way.' But nevertheless, if Wales, Scotland and Ireland are left out of the picture, as I have reluctantly decided they must, there is much which does apply across the board.

By the early nineteenth century, a long slow process of change had been completed. Widespread enclosures of common lands had replaced the old open-field farming with farms with settled lands, turning the husbandman into a farmer and the peasant into a wage labourer. Smaller farms were being steadily swallowed up into large ones. Historians in recent years, reacting to over-simplifications of the past, have tended to play down the harsh consequences of enclosure, arguing that the majority of labourers had little or no access to land before enclosure, and noting instead the greater efficiency and profitability which it brought to farming. But little of that profit accrued to the farmworker, and by 1830 the rural workforce, especially in the southern counties and East Anglia, was in open revolt. The 'Swing' riots of 1830 were fuelled by desperation at low living standards, low wages and underemployment caused by a stagnant demand for labour but rapidly increasing population.

This unrest was harshly put down, with many men hung or deported on hearsay evidence. It was not until the 1870s that the simmering unrest which had fuelled the Swing rioters found new and more eloquent expression in the trade union agitation lead by Joseph Arch. In the years between, the social divisions of rural life, hardened by the violent feelings which flamed on all sides in 1830, widened. The Game laws, which reserved all game down to the last rabbit for the 'sport' of the rich, were administered with rigour and severity by the very people whom they benefited. This manifest injustice, more than the restriction on the villagers' diet, was the worst aspect of the situation, for it created a whole criminal sub-class whose only crime was poaching or intent to poach. In the early 1840s, Alexander Somerville met a labourer at St Giles', the seat of the Earl of Shaftesbury, who roundly abused all 'lords, and squires, and parsons, and farmers' as 'a precious lot o' hard screws on a poor man, the whole lot of you'.

This perception must have been shared by many who lacked the independence to express it. Landlords and employers possessed an immense degree of influence over every aspect of the workforce's life from their morals to their very clothing: a labourer who aspired to anything better than corduroy trousers would soon be rebuked for getting above his station. As many cottages were 'tied', a labourer who lost his job often also lost his home; small tenant farmers were in a similarly insecure position if they offended their landlords.

This problem was most acute in what are known as 'close' villages. These were villages with one or two large landowners who controlled the population to below that needed to work the land, and exercised tight control over the morals and behaviour of their tenants. In some cases, landowners pulled down empty cottages and refused to build new ones, as a way of limiting poor law liability by shifting paupers into neighbouring 'open' villages. The open villages were larger, sprawling affairs, often overpopulated, burdened with excessive poor rates, but supporting numerous smallholders, craftsmen and tradesmen. Cottage rents were much lower in the close villages, and cottages were sometimes better maintained; rents in open villages were higher and accommodation was often jerry-built. The high level of social control exercised by the squires of close villages ensured that malcontents and troublemakers either left of their own accord or were expelled into the open villages, many of which were rough places.

Every form of dissent, notably in religion, was banished from the close village, even under the most well-meaning landlord. There was no non-conformist chapel, for instance, in the 'model' villages of Lockinge and Ardington built by the paternalistic Lord Wantage, whose wife expected regular attendance at church from her tenants. When G.F. Millin visited Lockinge for the liberal *Daily News* in 1891 he found it in many respects 'Arcadia realised'. He wrote of it as 'a self-contained world in which nobody is idle, nobody is in absolute want, in which there is no squalor and hunger, while in the midst of it all is the great house of Lockinge the beautiful home of Lord and Lady Wantage, always ready to play the part of benevolent friends to all who need their help.' But he noted that 'as a means of keeping the control and management of the people by the aristocracy nothing could possibly be better.' He quoted a labourer as saying that 'They daren't blow their noses over at Ardington without the bailiff's leave.'

Lord Wantage's concern for the welfare of his tenants ran deep. Lockinge had a reading room and a well-managed public house, its cottages had gardens, there were allotments close to the village, the village store was a profit-sharing co-operative, and – though wages were the average ten shillings a week – a bonus system was operated which gave the workers a small share in the farm profits. Generally speaking, the squire was a much remoter and less beneficent figure than this.

It was this lack of independence which accounted for what Richard Jefferies called 'the desultory nature of village life', and which, together with the slow pace and isolation of rural life produced the characteristic speech of the old-style countryman abashed by his betters. He spoke, wrote Augustus Jessopp, 'in what may be called the dubitative or approximating style':

> He is always feeling for what he has to say through a maze of tangled expletives, qualifications, retractations, and corrections. He knows he is not sure of his ground, that he has not said what he had in his mind; he is afraid of the consequences of articulate speech, and expects to gain something by silence.

This cowed inarticulacy in the face of authority confirmed the Victorians in their idea of the rural labourer as a lumpen yokel figure they called 'Hodge'. Hardy, who knew how pungently expressive local speech was in its own context, protested strongly against this 'pitiable picture' of 'a degraded being of uncouth manner and aspect, stolid understanding, and snail-like movement.' On close inspection, this 'dull, unvarying, joyless' figure cease to exist:

> He has become disintegrated into a number of dissimilar fellow-creatures, men of many minds, infinite in difference; some happy, many serene, a few depressed; some clever, even to genius, some stupid, some wanton, some austere; some mutely Miltonic, some Cromwellian; into men who have private views of each other..; who applaud or condemn each other; amuse or sadden themselves by the contemplation of each other's foibles or vices; and each of whom walks in his own way the road to dusty death.

It is impossible to write such a book as this without referring magisterially to 'the labourer', but no such composite figure existed. The working and living conditions of this class were so impoverished that it is well to be reminded that fun, laughter and tenderness are not confined to the comfortable, and that each life was an individual struggle with circumstance. Many men, for instance, bringing alert minds to their daily tasks, became through sheer observation fine naturalists; life in the open air had its compensations for men to whom the alternative was to breathe the noxious air of the Victorian slums.

In 1851 there were 1,284,000 male and 199,000 female farmworkers in England, representing a fifth of the total workforce. This was the highpoint of agricultural employment, and the figure gradually declined through the second half of the century, both as an actual figure and as a proportion of the working population. By the close of Victoria's reign, only one in eleven workers was employed in agriculture. The rough equation was that arable farming (as in the south and east) required one worker per 25 or 30 acres, while pastoral farming (as in the north and west) required only one man per 50 or 60 acres.

Another striking regional variation in the Victorian countryside was that, because higher industrial wages in the north established a 'floor' for agricultural wages, labourers in the north were better paid by about 3 shillings a week or 37%. Except for a brief rise in the 1870s, wages in the south remained around 9 or 10 shillings, sometimes as low as 7 or 8 shillings in depressed areas such as Wiltshire. These were supplemented by free or cheap cottage accommodation, usually a beer allowance, and sometimes other allowances in kind (such as fuel). In the north, farmworkers tended still to live in the farmhouse, in the old-fashioned way, eating at the farmer's table. Such differences, as well as different ways of calculating and supplementing wages, make precise comparisons of living standards almost impossible.

By the 1850s, a number of powerful forces for change were at work in the countryside. First, there was increasing mechanisation, which replaced labourers with machines. Second, there was the lure of emigration or alternative employment, for instance on the railways. Third, better roads, better transport and better education were opening up the enclosed village world to outside influences as never before. Fourth, there was the agricultural slump which began in the 1870s and continued for the rest of the century, leaving farming in the sorry mess recorded in Rider Haggard's survey of *Rural England* in 1901. This slump was essentially caused by a series of poor harvests combined with cheap imports from America and elsewhere which, in the absence of the protective Corn Laws against which men like Alexander Somerville had campaigned, caused all agricultural prices, but especially wheat, to fall. Farmers and landowners who had spent large amounts of money on new drainage in order to follow the fashion for intensive or 'high' farming could not get a return on their outlay. There was a consequent move away from arable farming, and towards pastoral, which required fewer workers.

All these forces were to affect the village, and the villager, radically.

RATHER WORK THAN PLAY

✎ THE VILLAGE CHILD ✐

When I do not work, I go out to play. I had rather work than play;
you get most victuals when you work.
JAMES ORTON, A KENT BOY, 1843

THE LIFE OF the Victorian village child was dominated by the same stern necessities as that of its parents. Children were expected to start contributing to the family income at the earliest possible age: girls were set to learn the art of making straw plait for the hat industry, for instance, as young as three.

Although the Agricultural Children Act of 1873 prohibited the employment of children under the age of eight, and was intended to enforce elementary school attendance until the age of twelve, it was a dead letter. Though the position of children gradually improved, many adults' memories of early childhood were to chime with those of Mrs Burrows, who recalled of her childhood in the fens in the 1850s:

> In the very short schooling that I obtained, I learnt neither grammar nor writing. On the day that I was eight years of age, I left school, and began to work fourteen hours a day in the fields, with from forty to fifty other children of whom, even at that early age, I was the eldest. We were followed all day long by an old man carrying a long whip in his hand, which he did not forget to use.

Parents would not have sent their children to work in such conditions if it were not vital to the family's survival. William Cobbett wrote of his delight in 'the excessive fondness of the labouring people for their children.' But the Sussex man who told Cobbett that he did not care how many children he had because, 'God never sends mouths without sending meat', was proved horribly wrong in the harsher Victorian years which followed. Hardy wrote to Rider Haggard that, 'as a child I knew by sight a sheep-keeping boy who, to my horror, shortly afterwards died of want, the contents of his stomach at the autopsy being raw turnip only.'

Such a diet may be contrasted with the 'dull and monotonous' nursery meals remembered by Lady Eleanor Acland in the 1880s:

> For breakfast we had a boiled egg each on Sundays, Tuesdays and Thursdays, bread and milk on the other four . . . followed by a slice of bread and butter. For dinner, roast meat and boiled potatoes; milk puddings in winter, and in summer a shape, which we called 'co' mo',' accompanied by stewed fruit – nearly always prunes, apples, or rhubarb; for tea, two slices of bread and butter, one of bread and jam, and one bit of sponge-cake; for supper, eight 'animal' biscuits, and one third of a big jug of milk.

In the absence of any effective method of contraception except total abstinence, families were large. The average farmworker's family was perhaps not much larger than in the country as a whole, but there were some very numerous families. The diaries of the Relieving Officer George Dew, for instance, note the case in 1870 of Sarah and Samuel Powell of Bucknell, in their early fifties, who had had twenty-three children. Of these, only seven survived.

In this situation, the finer sentiments of parenthood could become blunted. Although most parents loved their children, and mourned the loss of those that died, in darker times children could seem mere 'squalling babbies', extra mouths to feed, and the sooner they were earning money, the better. Richard Jefferies writes of the labouring classes:

> They seem to look upon their offspring as merely slaves. They are fond of them in their way, no doubt, but the law of implicit obedience is maintained by dint of blows and stripes. The children are kicked, punched and thrashed perpetually.

This reliance on physical correction was not, of course, confined to the poor. The same could be said, in more temperate but no less painful terms, of many middle and upper class homes.

No doubt some labouring families were brutal to their children, but one must remember that corporal punishment was almost the only punishment available to them: there were no treats or presents to withhold, and they had neither the time nor the mental framework to sit down and reason with unruly offspring. A spry child, such as the Essex lad Isaac Mead in the 1860s, could sidestep even that. He recalled:

> If I was in any danger of contact with my mother, my method was to pick as nice a bunch of wild flowers as I could possibly get, and as I arrived home I would say, 'Now, mother, how do you like these?' And should it be that the flowers did not ward off the punishment, the next course was a good sing-song. I have heard my mother laugh in later years that 'twas no use to thrash me, for it only made me sing.

Cottage children had few or no toys. Edwin Grey remembered from Harpenden, Herts in the 1870s, clothes peg or rag dolls, a simple wooden Noah's ark, windmills acquired from the rag and bone man, and also penny monkeys on sticks and squealing ducks which were purchased at the Statute or 'Stattice' fairs; at school, children played with tops, marbles, and metal buttons thrown at a mark. But there were, of course, many games which needed no equipment. Grey remembered that:

> On winter nights we had a number of romping games whereby we kept ourselves warm, in most of which the girls also joined – 'Warrings', 'Bull in the Ring', 'Jump a little Nagtail', 'Here goes a Shot', 'I spy', and several other games now seldom if ever played. Summer nights the games 'Baseball', 'Tiggy, Tiggy Touchwood', 'Molly Peg', 'Nest Eggs', etc., besides, of course, cricket, for the boys of each group or colony of cottages, Bowling Alley, Hatching Green, Pimlico, etc., had their own little cricket club. The lads and girls also played at 'Shinney' on the Common; this game being played with knobbed sticks and a ball or maybe a wooden or cork bung from a beer barrel, the sticks being cut from the hedgerows.

In 1875, Francis Kilvert, rector of Langley Burrell in Wiltshire, noted two children at play in the dusk on the common field in front of some cottages, and reflected on 'the wealth of the child's imagination and capacity for enjoyment of trifles':

> One tiny urchin was carefully binding a handkerchief round the face of an urchin even more tiny than himself. It was Fred and Jerry Savine. 'What are you doing to him?' I asked Fred. 'Please, Sir,' said the child solemnly. 'Please, Sir, we'm gwine to play at blindman's buff.' The two children were quite alone. The strip of dusky meadow was like a

marsh and every footstep trod the water out of the soaked land, but the two little images went solemnly on with their game as if they were in a magnificent playground with a hundred children to play with.

Middle class children, brought up in a more leisured environment, had more sophisticated pleasures, though even these seem very simple by today's standards. George Sturt, whose father was a wheelwright and whose mother kept a newsagent's shop, remembered that:

> Our usual pastime was to sit round the light, prattling over our little jobs – my sisters at their needlework or doll-dressing, myself with a pair of scissors 'cutting-out' figures for scrap-books. We sometimes played games. And if the games involved a little dressing-up, so much the better.

Mary Cholmondely, whose father was Rector of Hodnet in Shropshire, recalled with pleasure how, 'He made a toy theatre, painted the scenery, and acted five-act plays with dolls. Mother wrote the plays and he "produced" them.'

Children of the parson, squire or other local grandee would have almost no contact with children outside their class, beyond perhaps accompanying their mother on visits to the sick or crippled with charitable bowls of soup. This was certainly so for Lady Eleanor Acland, who when she asked why she could not play with children in the village was firmly told that 'young ladies and gentlemen didn't play with village children because you never know what you might pick up.' She recalled:

> There was more fixity of class feeling, as about so many other things, in those days than there is now, and we were but little concerned with the children who lived in the farms and cottages round about our home, accepting (as did they) the then generally accepted notion that our lives and theirs were unconnected.

Instead of joining the village rough-and-tumble, she led a socially pure but very restricted life, at the severe beck and call of a grim nurse. Lessons were with her cousins at the vicarage.

The children of artisans, shopkeepers and small farmers were less cosseted; Geoffrey Robinson's uncles and aunts at Hedingham, while expected to do their share of hard work around their father's farm, ran, recalled Matilda, 'as wild as the wind' outdoors. Alison Uttley, the daughter of a Derbyshire tenant farmer, was brought up on an isolated farm in the Peak District, but trudged several miles to school with local villagers. Although, as she recorded in her memoir *The Country Child*, she was abashed by the roughness of the boys, she also enjoyed such homely pleasures as the 'peep-shows' which the children made in summer:

> 'A pin to see a peep-show'. The children cut open a door from an envelope, and hid behind a piece of glass a few flower-petals arranged in a design, a group of slender leaves of lad's love, with a circle of larkspur petals. The payment to see the wonder, to lift the paper curtain and peep, was a pin.

Besides such homely pleasures, the children's lives were very much brightened by the many calendar customs they observed through the year. At the simplest was something like Oak Apple or Shick Shack Day, 29 May, when the children wore oak leaves about their person, anyone failing to so do being liable for punishment such as being stung with nettles. Many of the customs involved begging for a dole from the better off sections of the community. Children in the villages round London used to make pebble and shell grottoes on 25 July and beg passers-by to 'please remember the grotto'; on May Day, children in many villages made flower garlands which they paraded round the village, singing some such rhyme as that collected at Shilton in the Upper Thames:

> Good morning, ladies and gentlemen, it is the first of May,
> And we are come to garlanding because it is new May Day;
> A bunch of flowers we have brought you, and at your door we stay,
> So please to give us what you can, and then we'll go away.

As both parents worked a long and gruelling day, the children were left very much to their own devices, often locked out of their homes. The oldest girl would be set to look after her siblings, and oversee their play in the dusty roads, hedges and ditches in which they spent their days. Even the smallest fingers could be useful at such times as the acorn harvest, when farmers paid good money for acorns with which to feed their pigs, but there were some carefree times. Richard Jefferies writes:

> In spring is their happiest time. The joy of life – the warm sunshine and pleasant breeze of spring – is not wholly lost upon them, despite their hard fare, and the not very affectionate treatment they receive at home. Such a girl may then be seen sitting under a willow beside the brook,

with her charges around her – the little brother that can just toddle, the baby that can but crawl and crow in the green fresh grass. Between them lies a whole pile of flowers – dandelion stems made into rings, and the rings joined together so as to form a chain, rushes plaited, blue-bells, cowslips tied up in balls, and cowslips loose, their yellow petals scattered over the sward.

Such children's schooling was wayward and irregular, and largely irrelevant to the lives they would afterwards lead. Before the 1870 Elementary Education Act, which guaranteed an elementary place for every child, village education had been entirely unsupervised, and many village schools were essentially child-minding institutions, like the old Dame schools, rather than places of education. Some villages had funded parochial schools, and in many the Church of England clergyman had raised the funds for a so-called National or church school. The level of teaching in these places varied from negligible to excellent; in the days before the first certificated teachers in 1846, and still for many years after that, parents and children had to accept the luck of the draw in their teachers. Some were competent. Joseph Arch, the agricultural labourers' leader, attributed his firm grounding in the basics of the 'three Rs' to his schoolmaster, a 'sensible and practical' man who, although the school was 'one of the parson kind', 'flatly refused to waste his time and ours over the catechism and other such educational lumber.'

The catechism loomed large in most schools, and involved the children in learning by rote the approved answers to such meta-physical nonsense as 'Who is your Ghostly enemy?' Vicars made quite a game of recording the supposedly foolish answers they received to such questions, but these little exchanges have often acquired a bitter ring over time. To the question above, for instance, a child answered, 'Granum, sir.' 'Your grandmother? Nonsense, now –' 'But she is sir, because she larrups me so.'

Geoffrey Robinson's account of catechising in Hedingham paints a vivid picture of the scene:

> Hedingham was a church school. Therefore the catechism had to be known by heart, and once a year the Rector appeared in his frock-coat and high flat-topped felt hat to examine the school in scripture. Then Mr Palfreyman, who otherwise feared no one, edged round behind him, so that he could mouth the answers for the duller pupils, for he dared not risk the school being denied its grant from the church. The

Reverend Mr Smith had never married and slept with his maids instead. My grandfather used to say that he gave them 'three services a week'. Consequently, between searching questions on the catechism, the parson cast his eye over the adolescent girls in the back row for likely recruits to his rectory harem.

Many children were not so lucky as Joseph Arch, or the well-taught pupils of Hedingham. The pages of Royal Commissions of enquiry into rural life are full of children who do not know the names of the months, or have never heard of Jesus Christ. One Kentish woman testified that she was still 'a dunce . . . about the months in the year':

> I've always regretted not going to school. My children all go . . . My boy (William) didn't go to school till he was 10, then he went altogether. He's no scholar; he's a bad boy, would never learn, no schooling is any good to him. He could write nicely when he left school; he can read but he cares nothing about it, he doesn't learn a bit what it means.

There were always bright spots. For instance at the English Presbyterian School at Wooler, Northumberland, in 1867, four boys were reported to be learning Latin: the sons of a gamekeeper, a shepherd, a skinner of sheep and of the widow of a railway porter. There were, too, efforts by the poor themselves to establish night schools, such as the one run by John Brudenell, 'a common farm labourer', at Irchester in Northamptonshire. He told the 1867 Royal Commission:

> There used to be no school here. I used to teach them in the winter. They did not know where to go, and they wanted some learning, so I said, 'I'll teach you.' That was 28 years ago. About six came to my cottage to be taught. That went on for two winters. I took it up again about three years ago, because there was no school. The boys' friends asked me. I let them come to my house. Seventeen was the most I had; I had no room for more. I might have had many more if I had had room. They paid me 1d per week, and found their own lights. They each brought a candle in turn. I taught them to read, write and spell. They came very regularly for about four months. They were all boys. Their friends wanted them to learn. They used to come from 7 to 8. They got on uncommon well some on 'em. Many of them did not know how to make a stroke when they came, and could write their names fair when they left. There are a good many now who want to learn, but they don't like to go to the school, because there are not enough people to teach 'em. A man cannot manage more than a score; 30 or 40 go to the

night school now. I think it would be a very good thing if a law said you shall not send your boy to work unless he can read and write.

Occasionally, employers did make some efforts at education. For instance the Norfolk lady farmer, Louisa Mary Cresswell, organised a Sunday school each winter for the boys who worked on the farm, helped by her son:

> I suppose they liked it or they would not have walked down from the village through slush and snow, and no constraint was put upon them to come, and they had nothing but a piece of bread and cheese before they went home; even the under gamekeeper's boys asked leave to join it though they lived a long way off.

However she disapproved deeply of 'this new education craze', and thought village children should start full-time work at the age of nine or ten at the latest.

The 1870 Act required every parish to provide a school, and where none existed, School Boards were created to raise the necessary funds. The composition of these boards varied. Sometimes they were merely a group of farmers whose main concern was keeping expenditure from the rates as low as possible. But, especially in villages with a strong dissenting or non-conformist element, the effect of the School Boards was to radically shift power over education away from the Church of England. In the Leicester village of Oadby, for instance, the reprobate poacher James Hawker was for a time a member of the School Board.

The parsons fought a sharp rearguard action to retain what control they could: Joseph Arch describes the system operational in Barford, where parents were required to obtain a ticket from the parson to admit a boy to school, or from his wife for a girl. Arch challenged this, and won, but a similar flexing of muscles must have occured in parishes up and down the country.

The Education Acts of 1876 and 1880 required full-time attendance at school from the age of five to ten, and part-time till the age of fourteen unless the child had attained a certificate of exemption by passing the simple examination for Standard IV. Few cottage children advanced beyond Standard V. Even so, there was much absenteeism. At crucial moments of the agricultural year, such as harvest, or hop-picking in Kent, most of the children would be kept from school, and although it was possible for parents to be fined small sums for withholding their children from school, this was not applied strictly. Rider Haggard, who was a magistrate, discusses some of the problems involved in School Board prosecutions in his *A Farmer's Year*:

> Magistrates are frequently blamed – for the most part by doctrinaire enthusiasts or persons who have little practical acquaintance with the conditions under which the poor live – because they are not more severe upon this class of offence. Yet in many instances the circumstances brought before them are so piteous that they feel it would be nothing short of wicked to add to the misery of the persons concerned by a fine to be levied on such belongings as they still possess. Sometimes the husband is a drunkard, and the mother keeps the child at home to mind the little ones while she goes out to work in the fields to find bread to put into the mouths of all of them. Sometimes she is sick – very likely confined of the twelfth or thirteenth baby – and an elder girl who has not yet passed her appointed standards is forced to take her place for the time being; and so on, with variations.

For all that, many labourers literally hungered for education for their children, finding precious pennies to pay school fees to give their children a better start, until elementary school attendance fees were abolished in 1891. They recognised that, in the phrase of a labourer who was bailiff to the Rev. Burney of Wickham Bishop in Essex, 'A pen earns an easy loaf.' On the other hand, many also resented that their children were being educated as if they were going to be clerks in an office rather than workers on the land. There was very little attempt to interest children in the history or the skills of their own communities.

Inevitably, many farmers saw little point in educating the children of labourers above their station, and many objected, too, to their own children sitting side by side with those of their employees. Children of the well off were sent away to school, and even the children of the manor played surprisingly little part in village life.

For many children their first employment was, like Hardy's Jude, in scaring away the crows from the farmer's crops. This was so, for instance, for Joseph Ashby of Tysoe:

> From the time he was nine Joseph would spend long, lonely days in school vacations and on Saturdays scaring crows off the short, green corn. He had a wooden clapper, but if he saw no one for hours he took to shouting so as to hear a human voice. This method had another convenience; you couldn't cry while you shouted.

There were a variety of bird-starving cries. One went:

> Hi! Shoo all o' the birds
> Shoo aller birds
> Shoo aller birds
>
> Out of master's ground
> Into Tom Tucker's ground
>
> Out of Tom Tucker's ground
> Into Tom Tinker's ground
>
> Out of Tom Tinker's ground
> Into Luke Collis' ground
>
> Out of Luke Collis' ground
> Into Bill Vater's ground
>
> Hi! Shoo aller birds
> Kraw! Hoop!

The crow-scarers passed about ten hours a day in complete isolation, amusing themselves by cutting labyrinths in the turf and 'carving on gates, trees, or sticks'. Whenever anyone passed they would ask plaintively 'Plase, Master, can ye tell us wot toime it is?'

An interested and sympathetic observer, The Hon. and Rev. Sidney Godolphin Osborne, observes, however, that 'I think the importance of their trust, and the knowledge that they are earning wages, goes far to lighten the effect of the monotony of their employment.' Children were pleased to earn money for their families: one girl told a commissioner proudly, 'Father said I did more work last summer than I had any summer before.'

While crow-scaring or 'tenting' with its long hours of isolation provided many children with their bitterest hours of labour, it was only one of many tasks alloted to children as young as six. Others included stone picking, bean setting, weeding, and gleaning after harvest.

Children as young as eight or nine were set to the plough. Ten-year-old Albert Merritt of Almondsbury in Essex, whose case was reported in 1867, was by no means unusual:

> Has been working for farmer Carter; earned 3s a week; drove the plough; liked school better; found himself tired with his day's work; got so much walking. Would leave home at 5 or 5.30 a.m.; go to farm, help to clean out his stable and get the horses ready. Then got his

32

breakfast, which he had brought with him, bread and cheese, and half a pint of cider, allowed by his master. Went with the horses on the land, at work till noon; then got a quarter of an hour for dinner, bread and cheese and cider. Kept on ploughing till three, then took the horses home, that would perhaps occupy half an hour. When they got home to farm, the ploughman went in to get his dinner in the house while he looked after the horses, fed them; helped to cut the chaff. Did not get home till 7 o'clock; had his supper, potatoes and bacon, with nothing to drink. Goes to bed at 8 o'clock.

These early years following the plough left their mark. Many commentators noted their effect on the gait and carriage of the adult country labourer; as a doctor from Witney in Oxfordshire put it, 'when they get to be about 50 they go at the knees.' Richard Jefferies is characteristically acute:

> The labourer's muscle is that of a cart-horse, his motions lumbering and slow. His style of walk is caused by following the plough in early childhood, when the weak limbs find it a hard labour to pull the heavy nailed boots from the thick clay soil. Ever afterwards he walks as if it were an exertion to lift his legs.

In his *The Whistler at the Plough* (1852), Alexander Somerville recounts a conversation with a sixteen-year-old ploughboy on a large farm near Abingdon, who survived on a diet of bread and lard for a wage of three shillings a week, sleeping in the stable loft with four other hired lads. On hearing that the boy's bedclothes were changed just once a year, Somerville asked him, 'Don't you find your bed disagreeable?':

> Do I! I bees too sleepy. I never knows nought of it, only that I has to get up afore I be awake. and never get into it afore I be asleep. I be up at four, and ben't done work afore eight at night.

Truly in such circumstances it called for a special ebullience of spirit to whistle at the plough, perhaps a chorus celebrating the ploughboy's skill:

> For 'tis hark the little ploughboy gets up in the morn,
> Whoop along, jump along,
> Here drives the ploughboy with Spark and Beauty Berry,
> Good luck Speedwell, Cherry,
> For it's whoop a long,
> For we are the lads that can keep along the plough,
> For we are the lads that can keep along the plough.

Edwin Grey noted that the Hertfordshire boys hired out as early as they could as farm lads. By living at the farms, they made more room at home.

If a boy had ambitions beyond labouring, he might try to get indentured as an apprentice, but by the time this happened, he would already have a fairly wide work experience. Joseph Millott Severn is a case in point. He was born and brought up in the Derbyshire mining village of Codnor, and on his seventeenth birthday became apprenticed to a joiner, to learn carpentry, wheelwrighting, undertaking and building, even though this meant a drop in wages from 24*s* to 8*s*. He had first begun working at the age of seven or eight, helping in the evenings after school, on Saturdays and in the school holidays at silk-winding at a farthing a skein. Then he worked as a farmer's boy, and gives a vivid account of the farmhouse fare:

> The cheese we had to eat was so hard that one's teeth would have stood no chance had they not been strong and good. The brown bread was weeks old, and almost as hard as the cheese. We had cold tea or oatmeal water to drink, and sometimes a bit of fat bacon with the bread; in the evening on our return to the farm, we had bread and milk in old fashioned wooden bowls, while sitting at a long bench in the farmer's kitchen in the twilight.

At the age of twelve, he started work in an ironstone mine, working twelve-hour shifts underground, an experience which ensured that his early farm work, taxing as it was, remained an idyllic memory. He started out to work before 5 a.m., returned home after 7 p.m., snatched supper and a wash and went straight to bed. His account of his father waking him for work in the mornings is one of the tenderest pictures we have of the parent-child relationship in a cottage family:

> One seemed not to be in bed long before being awakened at a quarter past four; and oh! the patience my poor father had in coaxing me to get up – he always did this to save mother getting up so early – telling me all sorts of tales, singing little ditties to me, telling me only another day, when it would be short day and money day, and then Sunday, and all such similar things, and eventually gently sprinkling my face with water; and after a while I would be sufficiently awake to understand that it was again getting-up time. Meanwhile father had got hot water boiling in the kettle, and my breakfast ready, put the cold tea left from the day before in a big tin bottle, and packed up a 'snap-bag' of plain food to last me the day.

By the time of his apprenticeship, Severn had also worked in a coal mine and as a stockinger or framework knitter.

Except in the notorious agricultural 'gangs' of Norfolk, girls were rarely as hard-worked as this; or, rather, their tasks came chiefly in the home, helping with housework and looking after their younger siblings; undergoing, as Richard Jefferies puts it, an 'education in the cares of maternity'.

About the age of twelve, many cottage girls went into service, initially for a year in what was called a 'petty place' in the house of some small tradesman, schoolmaster, bailiff or suchlike. Putting girls to domestic service was an economic necessity, but it also owed something to the need to find more room in overcrowded cottages. After the petty place, their mothers would try to get them a post as a scullery maid or tweeny in some large household, often many miles from home. Most sent money home, often as much as half their meagre wages, and returned home for their fortnight's holiday each year. Some would return to the village, perhaps to marry some local sweetheart; others went on to broader horizons.

Fourteen-year-old Ellen Brown, from Metheringham in Lincolnshire, interviewed in 1867, can speak for all:

> I'm in service. Went last year on the turnip land in the gangs. We first cleaned the turnips, and then topped and tailed them. I got 9d and 10d a day. I've been out three summers and two winters. It's very cold work on the turnip land; my clothes would freeze round me. We used to go at 7 in winter and leave off at 4. I never been to school; I can't read or write.

2

A WOMAN'S WORK

◄§ WOMEN'S WORKING LIVES §►

A man's work is from sun to sun,
A woman's work is never done.
TRADITIONAL

ARTHUR WELTON, WHO was born in 1884, told George Ewart Evans, 'I recollect the women, they were always busy: they were never idle. There was always work to do.' As Kate Mary Edwards put it, 'if life were hard for the men, it were harder still for the womenfolk.'

In one folk song, the husband tells the wife that she does no work:

> He said: you lazy hussy
> Indeed you must confess,
> For I'm a-tired o' keeping you
> In all your idleness.
> But the woman she made him answer
> Saying: I work as hard as you.
> Then I will just run through the list
> What a woman has to do.
>
> *Chorus* So men if you would happy be,
> Don't grumble at your wife so,
> For no man can't imagine what
> A woman has to do.

Here's six o'clock each morning,
Off to your work you do go,
Here's eight arise and light the fire
And the bellows for to blow.
I have to set the tea things
And get the kettle boiled,
Besides you know, I have to work
And dress the youngest child.

Here's four times a day
Your wants for to employ,
Here's breakfast, dinner, tea and supper,
We have to stew and fry.
I have to shake and make the bed
And sweep the rooms also,
I have to dust the windows
And empty the chamber po.

It was to the women that the burden of running the home and looking after the children fell, and this in itself, in the days of large families and before the days of electricity, running water and labour-saving devices, was back-breaking work. In addition, food and clothing had to be provided from a wage scarcely equal to the task, and the way in which cottage women managed to make do won the admiration of all who observed it. On 26 November 1854, for instance, The Rev. Benjamin John Armstrong, vicar of East Dereham,

> Preached on the discipline of the body and drew a strong picture of the praiseworthy efforts of the female poor in clothing their families – the great need of clothing when so many 'gangs' of women and children work in the fields. It is astonishing how the poor contrive to live.

The 1843 Report of the Poor Law Commissioners on the Employment of Women and Children in Agriculture includes a table of the income and expenditure of an agricultural labourer's family in the village of Bolton Percy, near York, which shows how little room for manouevre such women had. It lists 'the vareas expinces belonging to Housekeeping for seven in famale; kept by Joseph and Jane Allen. Begun March 1, 1841; ended February 28, 1842.' Income amounted to £50 12s 6d; expenditure, confined to essential items, was £49 8s 9d.

The cares of the home were by no means women's only responsibility. Most women also worked to supplement their husband's meagre income, either in the fields – though this practice declined throughout our period except in special cases such as Northumberland – or in the home; there was always less farming work for women in pastoral areas.

The Norfolk 'gang' system which Armstrong mentions was only one of many means by which women and children were employed in agricultural work, but it is one worth examining in some detail. Joseph Arch described it thus:

> There were private gangs and public ones; small ones and large ones; fixed ones and wandering ones. Sometimes the gang would consist of one man and three or four children working under him; they would go turnip-singling and bean-dropping. Sometimes there would be a mixed gang of men and women weeding and picking 'twitch'; some would consist of women only. The potato gangs would be among the largest. You would see a line of women and children of all ages placed along a furrow at irregular distances . . . Such a gang would frequently number as many as seventy, and there would be a man walking up and down behind them superintending. Generally he was a rough bullying fellow, who could bluster and swear and threaten and knock the youngsters about and browbeat the women, but who was nothing of a workman himself. Pea-picking gangs were generally very large, consisting of four and five hundred women and children.

As described by Arch, Richard Heath and other sources, the gang workers existed in a state of virtual slavery to the gangmaster. This was particularly so for the children. Although the Gangs Act of 1867 prohibited the employment of children below the age of eight in a public gang, it did not apply to the private gangs which worked for one farmer rather than hiring out to the best bidder. Samuel Peeling, a Norfolk labourer told the Poor Law Commission of 1843:

> I have a daughter, turned 11, has worked 2 years along with the gang. Pulling turnips is very back-breaking work; she's too young to pull turnips; she don't often pull 'em; the men pull and the girls set 'em up . . . I'm forced to let my daughter go, else I'm very much against it. I earn nothing myself; she does not like it at all, she hears so much blackguard bad language; and she's never used to hearing that at home. She has complained of pain in her side very often; they drive them along – force them along – they make them work very hard.

The complaint about bad language was frequently made, and gang work, like working in the fields generally, was felt to put young women morally at risk. Miss Sculfer, a labouring woman of Castle Acre, Norfolk, testified in 1843:

> I have six children; three girls and three boys; my two eldest girls go out – most to my grief that I am obliged to send them. They worked for Mr Fuller (the chief gang-master) more than for anyone else . . . Fuller works boys and girls together . . . The lads pull turnips and the girls set them up after them. It's my belief that it's the ruin of them. They never settle to anything after it. My eldest girl has a thorough dislike to it. She almost always goes crying to her work. She would almost rather do anything than it. The worst place she could get anywhere, poor thing. I wish I knew of any place I could get for her. I'm sure I don't know what to do.

Miss Churchman added of Fuller, 'I know there's scores of girls as he's ruined: some of the gangsmen are as big blackguards as there is anywhere.'

Arch calls the women who worked in the gangs 'unnatural': 'rough and coarse and bold'. In part this reflects an imbibed middle class standard of decorous femininity, which was offended by the dress and manners of field women, but there is no doubt that the gang system was iniquitous. John Todd, overseer of one of Fuller's gangs, said, 'I believe that, owing to the gang-system, 70 out of 100 girls are very impudent girls – prostitutes.'

Elsewhere, field women often worked in groups, and relieved the monotony of the work with chaff and banter. As one Surrey woman told Arthur Munby in 1864: 'When a lot of women get together it's the pleasantest, for then there's company; but often we work alone – yesterday I was in this field alone, hoeing, from eight till five, all day.'

Hubert Simmons's *Stubble Farm* contains a scene of a group of field women bean-setting which nicely conveys the lively repartee of such occasions. The women tease 'old Jemmy' the bailiff, till he explodes:

> I don't want none of that gallus nonsense. Hold up your bag and take a peck of beans and get on planting; drat such silly talk as that. Master says you're not to get dropping too many beans in one hole, and if he catches any of you burying the beans in the ditch this year, he won't send you any beer. Last year some on ye shot a gallon of beans down one of the drains and drew the money for planting them, but I'm to tell you there will be somebody on the watch today, so you had better look out.

To which the answer is: 'Ah! That was the rats that carried them there; must have been.'

Thomas Hardy remembered with pleasure the field women of his childhood, and celebrated them in his poem 'At Middle-Field Gate in February':

> How dry it was on a far-back day
>   When straws hung the hedge and around,
> When amid the sheaves in amorous play
>   In curtained bonnets and light array
>   Bloomed a bevy now underground!

The closing decades of the century saw the virtual end of women working in the fields. While the census of 1851 showed 143,500 females employed in agriculture, in 1881 the figure was just 40,400. As Flora Thompson points out, the reputation of the 'lawless, slatternly' gangs of field women meant that by the 1880s many countrywomen were reluctant to do field work, though some still did, at a wage roughly half that of the men. A Kentish woman complained to Richard Heath: 'I go and do more than a man would, and yet they give a shilling instead of half a crown.'

The main exception to this retreat of women from the fields was the great communal effort of harvesting, which involved the whole family, men, women and children. As Richard Jefferies put it, 'The whole village lived in the field.' Generally the men would cut the corn, but, until the advent of the reaper-binder, it fell to the women to gather it and tie it into sheaves. This was so even after the mechanical reaper began to replace the scythe during the 1860s and 70s. Hardy's description in *Tess of the D'Urbervilles* cannot be bettered:

Her binding proceeds with clock-like monotony. From the sheaf last finished she draws a handful of ears, patting their tips with her left palm to bring them even. Then stooping low she moves forward, gathering the corn with both hands against her knees, and pushing her left gloved hand under the bundle to meet the right on the other side, holding the corn in an embrace like that of a lover. She brings the ends of the bond together, and kneels on the sheaf while she ties it, beating back her skirt now and then when lifted by the breeze. A bit of her naked arm is visible between the buff leather of the gauntlet and the sleeve of her gown; and as the day wears on its feminine smoothness becomes scarified by the stubble, and bleeds.

This division of labour was by no means fixed. In Tysoe, for instance, M.K. Ashby writes that:

> A dozen or maybe twenty reapers, largely women, would work in one field, with men following to tie up the sheaves and another group to set them in shucks.

Whatever the precise tasks alloted, harvest was certainly a time, as disapproving clergymen noted, for 'amorous play' as well as hard toil; again according to M.K. Ashby, 'there was talk and banter and flirting and yarn-spinning during the meals under the hedge.'

After the harvest, women and children scoured the fields, gleaning or 'leasing' the fallen ears. This immemorial right of the poor, enshrined in Mosaic law, came under some threat in the Victorian era, but remained almost universal. The small store of corn thus gathered made an important contribution to the family larder. A Wiltshire woman, Mrs Smart, describes it thus:

> I went out leasing this autumn for three weeks, and was very lucky: I got six bushels of corn. I got up at two o'clock in the morning, and got home at seven at night. My girls, aged ten, fifteen and eighteen, went with me. We leased in the neighbourhood, and sometimes as far as seven miles off. I have had thirteen children and have brought seven up. . . . In leasing, in bringing home the corn, I have hurt my head and been made deaf by it. Often, out of the hayfields, myself and my children have come home with our things wet through: I have gone to bed for an hour for my things to get a little dry, but have had to put them on again quite wet.

Aside from field work, there were employment opportunities for women as farm servants. In many ways this was just a more agricultural equivalent of service in any household, but girls who were skilled dairy maids could command high wages.

One specialised form of female farm servant was the Northumbrian 'bondager'. The Northumbrian labourers, known as 'hinds', had each to supply a female worker, often a daughter, to work as required. These women were employed on a wide variety of tasks. Arthur Munby, the barrister-poet who was obsessed by working women, gives a good picture of them:

> The bondager is strictly a servant in husbandry: she is hired to do outdoor work, and that only. If there is nothing to do in the fields, she often helps to do the dirty work of her master's house or her master's

master's; just as at Halton I saw the bondager busy at the washtub: but she is not bound to such trivial tasks: she may lounge about like a lad & whistle or snooze, until she be ordered afield. Once afield, she is put to any thing, except ploughing and ditching.

Munby approved of this hearty physical work, and one Northumbrian woman at least agreed with him, saying that, 'My daughter is much better since she worked out'; previously 'she was quite an invalid from poverty of blood' but 'now she is quite strong from working in the fields.' This woman was adamant that she would rather her daughter work in the field than go into service, but this was not the conventional view. Middle class observers were horrified at the unwomanly nature of field work, and felt that a training in service was much more suitable for country girls.

Ironically, girls who went into service were almost certainly more at risk from sexual predators than those in the fields. *My Secret Life*, the erotic autobiography of 'Walter' contains many descriptions of the bullying tactics he used in seducing servant girls, whom he regarded as legitimate prey. They could not complain or resist under threat of losing their 'character', without which they could not find another position. Nor was Walter alone in his behaviour. Joseph Ashby, for instance, was the illegitimate son of Elizabeth Ashby, a twenty-one year old maidservant, and the master of Idlicote House. At a lower social level, Geoffrey Robinson's grandfather, Edward Maitland Fisher, a Lincolnshire blacksmith-turned-tenant farmer, exercised a *droit de seigneur* over the family's servants, including the dairymaids. As Robinson explains:

> The butter churn was operated in the cream dairy, and from time to time my grandfather would go down the steps and take the maid from the rear as she bent over her work. It was typical of him that he should not want anyone in his employment to be idle, even while gratifying his desires.

Walter describes a conversation in his club about the usefulness of the dining room table:

> One night in the smoking room of my club, the conversation turning as usual upon women, I alluded to tables and wondered if every man present had used them. Ten men were present, and each said he had often times done so. One man, since dead, said he had shagged every servant he had on them. He was in the Foreign Office, not well off, and

kept but two servants. 'It's the safest place in the house,' said he, 'just before the cloth is laid. Your wife is most likely dressing, the cook cooking, and neither can interrupt you.'

In larger establishments, servant girls were perhaps more vulnerable to their fellow servants. Dearman Birchall's diary, for instance, describes the attempted rape of Elizabeth, a maid, in the laundry by another servant, Elwood. For this, Elwood was 'warned off', though, as he was the coachman and needed the following day, 'I delayed dismissing him until our return.'

There was an insatiable demand for country girls as servants; they were considered to be more pliable and more trustworthy than town girls. Richard Jefferies writes:

Ladies residing in the country are accustomed to receive periodical appeals from friends in town asking their assistance in procuring servants. So frequent are such appeals that there would seem to be a popular belief that the supply is inexhaustible. The villages are supposed to be full of girls, all ready to enter service, and, though a little uncouth in manner, possessed nevertheless of sterling good qualities.

Fortunately, the diaries of such a girl, Hannah Cullwick, a country girl who spent her life as a maid-of-all-work, have survived. She kept an account of her daily life to please Arthur Munby, to whom she was secretly married in an extraordinary relationship chronicled in Derek Hudson's *Munby: Man of Two Worlds*. The sheer drudgery of her repetitive and exhausting toil comes across in her description of a typical day:

Light the fire & clean'd the hearth & swept & dusted & clean'd 8 pairs of boots. Got breakfast up. Made the beds & emptied the slops. Clean'd & wash'd up the breakfast things. Swept the stairs & wash'd the lamp glasses & the things on the wash stands. Clean'd the knives and got dinner ready. Laid the cloth & took up the dinner & clean'd away. Clean'd the kitchen & passage & stairs & privy on my knees. Washed up in the scullery & clean'd the floor. Did some washing. Got tea; clean'd & wash'd up. Tied up the jam & got supper. Clean'd away & wash'd up & to bed.

Girls who took service often left after a number of years to marry, and resumed village life; Mrs Smart, whom I quoted on gleaning, had been a housemaid and then a cook before her marriage. A few tried to import into their daily lives some of the refinements with which their service had made them familiar, but to many, middle class manners must have seemed an irrelevance in a cottage home.

Even among the relatively well-to-do, housework without labour-saving devices was a considerable strain. The blacksmith's daughter Ann Staight, for instance, was essentially an unpaid skivvy for the male members of her family, and her diaries reveal a life nearly as hard-pressed as Hannah Cullwick's: 'Was up at 7, went straight to washing and kept on till 10 at night.' When Ann left home to work as a barmaid, she paradoxically found herself with much more leisure time than ever before.

Many cottage women earned money at home in one of the many sweated cottage industries, the principal being making straw plait for the hat trade, lacemaking, and gloving. Straw plait was an important industry in Bedfordshire, Bucks, Herts and Essex. Edwin Grey writes of his Hertfordshire village:

> The cottage industry of straw plaiting played a very important part in the village life of those days. Very many of the women and girls were engaged in it: some of the men and the lads were also good at the work, doing it at odd times, or in the evenings after farm work, but this home industry was always looked upon really as women's work, and although there were men and also lads who were wonderfully good at it, yet their plait hardly ever came up to the standard of that made by the women.

The craft was learnt as young as three years old, in plait 'schools' which were really just infant workshops. Jackie Saunders's little grocery store was one source of straws for plait, and he also bought plait to sell to merchants, in a system of barter for straws, plait and groceries in which no money changed hands. Other women bought their straw elsewhere and sold their plait in the open market in St Albans. Lucy Luck, a straw plait worker from Tring, Herts, has left a brief autobiography in which she describes the injurious effect on her health of this taxing work:

> I had sat night after night at work until eleven or twelve o'clock, using a rushlight candle, and my eyes had begun to get so bad that I could hardly see.

Lucy was born in 1848, and had been brought up in a workhouse after her father deserted the family, and at the age of nine went to work in a silk mill, making five yards of straw plait every night after work.

Then she went into service, and was sexually molested, so she turned once again to making plait.

Straw plait workers had a reputation for sexual looseness. László Gróf, in his study of the plait trade, *Children of Straw*, quotes a Major Burns on the subject, in 1842:

> They prefer plaiting, even now when the trade is so low, to the restraints of service; and having an extreme fondness for dress, they no doubt often resort to prostitution as a means of adding to their scanty earnings.

Gróf is sceptical about the extent of this immorality, which was also attributed to lacemakers. Certainly, lacemakers, fetchingly arranged in their cottage doorways, were in a prime position to take advantage of any opportunities that came their way. Walter is once again a useful authority. He recalls an escapade from his adolescence with his cousin Fred:

> One day we rode to the market town, and, putting up our horses, strolled about. Fred said, 'let's go and have a shove.' 'Where are the girls?' said I. 'Oh! I know, lend me some money.' 'I only have ten shillings.' 'That is more than we shall want.' We went down a lane past the town hall, by white-washed little cottages, at which girls were sitting or standing at the doors making a sort of lace. 'Do you see a girl you like?' said he. 'Why, they are lacemakers.' 'Yes, but some of them fuck for all that; there is the one I had with the last half-a-crown you lent me.' Two girls were standing, together; they nodded. 'Let's try them,' said Fred. We went into the cottage; it was a new experience to me. He took one girl, leaving me the other; I felt so nervous; she laughed as Fred (who had never in his life a spark of modesty) put his hands up her companion's clothes. That girl asked what he was going to give her, and it was settled at half-a-crown each.

Such sums, mere bagatelles to well-off boys like Walter and Fred, represented half a week's work to the girls. All the cottage industries were poorly paid, and often the close, intricate work was done in very bad light. Often, too, as in gloving, which was common in the West Country, the workers were required to buy their materials from the source to which they sold the finished goods, and were held responsible for spoilt material and imperfect work. By the turn of the century, all these cottage industries had virtually disappeared.

There were many other ways in which women could contribute to the family finances. There was a growth in large villages and country towns of small factories employing women. There were a wide variety of local handicrafts, and women could also sell cottage products such as eggs, poultry, fruit, jam and pies. Some took in washing, went charring, or, if skilled at needlework, did dressmaking.

Edwin Grey remembered a number of elderly spinsters at Harpenden, Herts in the 1870s, and their occupations: 'Polly Munt was an old lady who made and sold Vinegar Rock, a farthing a stick; Polly Elmer retailed bread, also doing a little mangling for a living; Betsy Belcher was an expert straw plaiter; Sally Bonstead worked in the fields.' Similarly, Isaac Mead remembered widows in his Essex village in the 1860s such as Mrs Sains who sold coal and took in washing and mangling, and Mrs Beard who acted as the village midwife.

Many female shopkeepers and midwives were widows. Agricultural labourers were prone to accidents causing death and disablement, and their widows were left to make do as best they could. Many workers paid a small subscription to an Oddfellows or other benefit society, as an insurance against falling sick for short periods, and Union members also received sick pay (which would be deducted from any Poor Law payments), but it was rare for employers' to carry any form of insurance, not being liable under the Employers' Liability Acts.

It can be seen that there were a wide variety of paid and unpaid tasks for women in the Victorian village. Much of the information we have about women workers is in the words of male observers, who often disapproved of women earning at all: work and wages both defeminised the gentle sex. Such a view totally discounted the immense courage and strength of character which village women brought to their dual tasks as wage earners and housewives, but it can be answered only with the ambiguous remark of Elizabeth Ashby when drawn into controversy: 'I could have a lot to say, but silence becomes me best.'

3

THE WHEAT IS BEAUTIFUL

❧ MEN'S WORKING LIVES ❧

The wheat is beautiful, but human life is labour.
RICHARD JEFFERIES

THE VICTORIAN VILLAGE was not a uniform organism, and the work which was carried out varied from area to area, community to community. Besides the purely agricultural villages, both arable and pastoral, there were for instance fishing villages, where the bulk of the population earned their living at sea, or on the shore by such means as winkling and cockling, and there were also, in the midlands and the north especially, many industrial villages. Lancashire, the West Riding of Yorkshire and Derbyshire, for instance, were dominated by the textile industry. The villages of the Black Country specialized in nail-making. There were mining villages, and communities based on activities such as brick-making and quarrying. One of the latter, Headington Quarry near Oxford, has been the subject of a fascinating study by Raphael Samuel, in his book *Village Life and Labour*. His detailed account of the working life of the 'quarry roughs' shows just how varied their skills and occupations were. He gives the following table of occupations in Headington Quarry as listed in the census of 1861:

Labourer	55	Brickmaker	5
Agric. lab.	16	Shopkeeper	4
Brickyard lab.	7	Carter	3
Quarryman's lab.	12	Shepherd	4
Mason's lab.	2	Farm boy	2
Mason	16	Hawker	8
Laundress	22	Servant	5
Quarryman	3	Nurse	2
Washerwoman	3	House propr.	2

Brick-burner, shepherd boy, teacher, clergyman, cordwainer, errand boy, pauper, gardener, lace-maker, coach-trimmer, farmer, whitesmith, gardener's labourer, porter, haggle-cart man, carpenter and wheelwright, charwoman – 1 each.

As Samuel notes, the term 'labourer' here 'is a misleading one and gives little idea of their actual work, or of the variety of skills which made up their livelihood.' These skills included bricklaying and brickmaking, stone-digging and an associated local rough stone-masonry known as 'nobbling', well-digging, land-draining, general handymanning, and also casual agricultural work.

Besides such clearly industrial villages, many villages boasted flour mills, bone mills, tanyards, quarries and so on. Nevertheless, the main business of the countryside, and thus of the villages, was agriculture. The precise nature of the work depended on the nature of the land and also on local tradition. In the Sussex Weald, for instance, the raising of spring chickens was a strong local industry: from the village of Heathfield in 1870, one carrier alone took 105,887 fowls to market in London. There were also localised crops, such as hops in Kent, and, in various areas including East Anglia and the West Country, the willow harvest. This, like hop-picking, employed men, women and children, and was an important element of the local economy. Richard Jefferies writes:

This willow harvest is looked forward to by the cottagers who live along the rivers as an opportunity for earning extra money. The quantity of osier thus treated seems immense, and yet the demand is said to be steady, and as the year advances the price of the willow rises. It is manufactured into all kinds of baskets – on farms, especially arable farms, numbers of baskets are used. Clothes baskets, market baskets, chaff baskets, bassinettes or cradles, etc., are some few of the articles manufactured from it. Large quantities of willow, too, are worked up unpeeled into hampers of all kinds. The number of hampers used in these days is beyond computation, and as they are constantly wearing out, fresh ones have to be made. An advantage of the willow is that it enables the farmer to derive a profit from land that would otherwise be comparatively valueless. . . . Almost any scrap or corner does for willow, and if properly tended it speedily pays for the labour.

The digging and preparation of the ground gives employment, and afterwards the weeding and the work required to clean the channels that conduct water round and through the bed. Then there is the cutting and the peeling, and finally the basket-making; and thus the willow, though so common as to be little regarded, finds work for many hands.

Substantial country businesses – for instance the agricultural suppliers Bradford and Sons, based in Yeovil – were founded on the withy trade.

Amid all this variety, the traditional work of the farm, growing crops and raising stock, went on in a form which, while slightly affected by new machinery and new theories of farming – especially intensive land drainage – had scarcely changed for centuries. In an essay of 1874, 'The Labourer's Daily Life', Richard Jefferies gave the readers of *Fraser's Magazine* a summary of the working day in Wiltshire. It was a picture which held true for farmworkers in many parts of England:

> The ordinary adult farm labourer commonly rises at from four to five o'clock; if he is a milker, and has to walk some little distance to his work, even as early as half-past three. Four was the general rule, but of late years the hour has grown later. He milks till five or half-past, carries the yokes to the dairy, and draws water for the dairymaid, or perhaps chops up some wood for her fire to scald the milk. At six he goes to breakfast, which consists of a hunch of bread and cheese as the rule, with now and then a piece of bacon, and as a milker he receives his quart of beer. At breakfast there is no hurry for half-an-hour or so; but some time before seven he is on at the ordinary work of the day. If a milker and very early riser, he is not usually put at the heavy jobs, but allowances are made for the work he has already done. The other men on the farm arrive at six. At eleven, or half-past, comes luncheon, which lasts a full hour, often an hour and a quarter. About three o'clock the task of milking again commences; the buckets are got out with a good deal of rattling and noise, the yokes fitted to the shoulders, and away he goes for an hour or hour and a half of milking. That done, he has to clean up the court and help the dairymaid put the heavier articles in place; then another quart of beer, and away home. The time of leaving off work varies from half-past five to half-past six. At ordinary seasons the other men leave at six, but in haymaking or harvest time they are expected to remain till the job in hand is finished, often till eight or half-past. This is compensated for by a hearty supper and almost unlimited beer.

These workers, regarded as unskilled labourers, had in fact to master a great many skills, and prided themselves in their ability to plough a straight furrow, to stack a rick, to use a sickle or a fagging hook. Those who had special skills – such as a particular knowledge of or affinity with animals, hurdle-making or plashing hedges – might gain both greater respect and better pay than their fellows.

They were employed in various ways: yearly, weekly, or as day labourers. Each method had its pluses and minuses. A day labourer had more independence and charging piece rates a good worker might make more than the average wage, but day labourers were liable not to be paid in bad weather. Hence those who worked as day labourers tended to be the most skilled, who could work at better rates, and the least skilled, who could get no other work. In some counties, such as Northumberland, yearly employment remained the rule; interestingly, this job security was felt by contemporary observers to make the Northumbrian 'hinds' more independent and upright than elsewhere, though with what truth it is hard to tell. Yearly labourers were usually taken on at statute or hiring fairs, and the deal sealed with a 'fastenpenny'. Fred Kitchen has left a vivid picture of a Yorkshire hiring fair in his autobiographical *Brother to the Ox*:

> We would stand about in groups, either in the market or the adjoining streets, until a farmer came along. After eyeing us over like so many oxen, he would say: 'Nah, my lads, any on yer seeking a place?' Being warmed up with good ale, we answered truculently, or offhandedly at least, that we didn't 'care a damn whether we got a place or not', and, 'What sort o' chap are yer wanting?'
>
> He would then say, 'wagoner', 'seconder', 'stable-lad', or 'cow-lad', according to which he wanted, and after singling out a man or boy that took his fancy would begin questioning him on his qualifications.
>
> 'Can ta ploo, thack, stack, and drive a binder, manage three horses abreast, and carry barley?' There was no end of questioning from both sides, for the 'fastening-penny' cut both ways, and neither man nor master could part company under a twelve-month without some lawful excuse.

Kitchen is describing the early years of the present century here, by which time farmers in many parts of the country were desperate for skilled workers, and the tables had been turned from forty years before, when there were more workers than jobs, and any 'truculence' would have gone down very badly. It was customary at many hiring fairs for the different workers to wear a token identifying their particular skill. Readers of *Far From the Madding Crowd* will remember how Gabriel Oak looks for work at the Casterbridge (Dorchester) hiring fair, where 'carters and waggoners were distinguished by having a piece of whip-cord twisted round their hats; thatchers wore a fragment of woven straw; shepherds held their sheep-crooks in their hands; and thus the situation required was known to the hirers at a glance.' When Gabriel fails to find work as a bailiff, he exchanges his overcoat for a smock-frock, purchases a sheep-crook, and thus lets it be known that he is available for work as a shepherd.

Patterns of hire varied in different parts of the country; a man might work for the same master all his life at weekly hire. The one major change in the second half of the nineteenth century was the rapid decline of the custom of farm servants living in. Where they still did, they no longer ate or mixed with the farmer's family, as in previous generations. As a broadside ballad complained:

> The farmer and the servants together used to dine,
> But now they're in the parlour with their pudding, beef and wine,
> The master and the mistress, their sons and daughters all alone,
> And they will eat the meat, and you may pick the bone.

At Edward Fisher's farmhouse in Hedingham (Waddingham), Lincolnshire, for instance, Geoffrey Robinson writes that there were still two living-in labourers in the 1890s:

> The two labourers fed in the kitchen at times different from the children, and both of them slept in one bed in the attic room that had an exclusive staircase from the kitchen. In this way they were effectively segregated from the family.

Robinson's *Hedingham Harvest* offers an excellent picture of the working life of a small farm at the turn of the century, to match that of Henry Rider Haggard's *A Farmer's Year*. In such books, or in surviving farmers' diaries such as those of James Stevens in Cornwall or John Simpson Calvertt in Oxfordshire, the sheer relentless grind of the year's work, and its vulnerability to vagaries of the weather and the market, come out very clearly. So, too, does the gulf between master and man even when, as in the Fishers' case, the family members also worked long hard hours on the land.

The tedium of much repetitive farm work was alleviated by a good deal of chaff, banter and cameraderie among the workers. Sometimes this could take on a threatening or cruel edge, but much it was good-humoured. In most villages, many labourers would by adulthood have acquired a nickname by which they would always be known. As Edwin Grey recalled:

> Many of the men bore nicknames – 'Clipper Weston', 'Slappy Twidell', 'Wacky Russell', 'Slenderman Heath', are some that I remember, names probably given to them in fun when boys, and they had stuck; these nicknamed men were seldom spoken or alluded to by their proper christian names.

Popularity was always assured for a good storyteller, and respect for a good worker.

The men had not only to be individually skilled, but to be able to work as a team. Many commentators marvelled at the finesse with which the labourers cut hay or corn. M.K. Ashby describes young Joseph Ashby's awed response to the precision and grace of mowers at haytime:

> The mowers worked six or nine in a row, each cutting a swath behind another. Their scythes went singing through the grass, and the triumph of the scythe and the rhythmic fall of the swath continued like a long, slow, sacred dance.

Sussex farmer William Wood remembered the mowers with delight both for their visual symmetry and for 'a stirring music they made – each scythe giving a slightly different note – each man however keeping the same time, for when one man stopped as his tool needed sharpening all the rest must stop and sharpen too.'

For visual splendour, and in importance, the corn harvest was the climax of the year. But visual splendour can deceive. W.H. Barrett recalled:

> The hell of the life was the harvest. You'd see some lovely paintings of men at harvest. Well! I was sixteen when I was told I had got to do me harvest, with the other men. . . . You'd start mowing at half-past six in the morning. You'd wipe the last lot of sweat off about half-past eight at night. . . . It were the first three days which were hell. After that your muscles got used to it. I seen a strong man stand up and howl like a child, especially if there were a lot of green stuff in the corn that made it harder.

The mowers kept to many old traditions, including in many areas choosing a 'King of the Mowers' from among the most skilled workers, who was their undisputed leader for the harvest period. He would negotiate a contract with the farmer for 'taking the harvest', which would specify exactly what the men were to do and how much they were to be paid for it. Mark Thurston, born at Larkfield on the Suffolk-Essex border in 1861, told C. Henry Warren about this custom:

> We were allus hired by the week, except at harvest. Then it was piece-wukk. I dessay you've heard of the 'lord', as we used to call 'im? Sometimes he was the horseman at the farm, but he might be anybody. His job was to act as a sort of foreman to the team of reapers – there was often as many as ten or a dozen of us – and he looked after the hours and wages and such like. He set the pace too. His first man was sometimes called the 'lady'. Well, when harvest was gettin' close, the 'lord' 'ld call his team together and goo an' argue it out with the farmer. They'd run over all the fields that had got to be harvested and wukk it out at so much the acre.

The Reverend Sabine Baring-Gould collected a West-country folk-song, 'All of a Row' which is worth quoting in full for its picture of the harvest scene, somewhat idealised but by no means far-fetched in its depiction of the general good humour of these teams of men at their back-breaking work. 'Brink' is a dialect word for stook; 'humming' means strong; the 'arrish' is the stubble. Here the 'Lord' is named the Catchpole:

> The corn is all ripe and the reapings begin,
> The fruits of the earth, O we gather them in;
> At morning so early the reaphooks we grind,
> And away to the fields for to reap and to bind.
> The foreman goes first in the hot summer glow,
> And sings with a laugh, my lads, of a row.
> *Then all of a row!*
> *Then all of a row!*
> *And tonight we will sing,*
> *Boys, all of a row.*

> 'We're in', says Catchpole, behind and before,
> 'We'll have a fresh edge and a sheaf or two more';
> The master stands back for to see us behind;
> 'Well done, honest fellows, bring the sheaves to the bind.
> Well done, honest fellows, pare up your first brink
> You shall have a fresh edge and a half pint to drink.'
> *Then all of a row! etc.*

And so we go on through the heat of the day,
Some reaping, some binding, all merry and gay,
We'll reap and we'll bind, we will whistle and sing,
Unflagging until the last sheaf we bring in;
It's all our enjoyment wherever we go,
To work and to sing, brothers, all of a row.
Then all of a row! etc.

Our day's work is done, to the farmhouse we steer,
To eat a good supper and drink humming beer;
We wish the good farmer all the blessings in life,
And drink to his health, and as well to his wife.
God prosper the grain for next harvest we sow,
And again in the arrish we'll sing, boys, hallo.
Then all of a row! etc.

The last line refers to the custom of 'halloing' money known as largesse from passers-by, which went into the company's drink fund.

One distinctive feature of harvest-time was the arrival in many parishes of teams of labourers from Ireland. These men were highly esteemed as good workers. Alison Uttley's *The Country Child* contains very happy memories of their annual visits to her father's farm in the Peak District, where they would be housed in an old barn. J.S. Fletcher also remembered them from Yorkshire. While they were 'quiet and peaceable', he writes, 'to the folk of the village they were as so many savages; the English labourers would never eat or drink with them.'

Of course not all villagers earned their living in the fields, though most would do fieldwork at harvest time. Many of the more stubbornly individualistic eaked out a living by rural odd-jobbing, for instance as carriers or rat-catchers. Mole-catchers earned money twice over, first for the death of the creature, and second for the sale of its skin. Describing the village of Harpenden, Hertfordshire, in the late 1860s and early '70s, Edwin Grey writes that while the cottagers were mostly agricultural labourers, they were also employed in 'gravel-digging, chalk-drawing, well-sinking, birch-making, and also a few at the local brewery and hat factory, and also a few men of higher calling.'

'Men of higher calling', such as solicitors and doctors, would have been found only in the larger villages, and mostly congregated in the country towns; the flavour of this rural bourgeoisie is best caught in

Richard Jefferies's *Hodge and his Masters,* which contains marvellous accounts of a country solicitor's office, a newspaper, a bank and a county court, but these centres of power and learning are perhaps just as narrowly but completely outside the scope of a book on 'village life' as they were outside the world of the villager.

The true village middle class was not made of such men, but rather of farmers, craftsmen and tradesmen: blacksmiths, wheelwrights, carpenters, shoemakers, potters, chairmakers, shopkeepers. These men banded together with a strong sense of mutual self-interest and village hierarchy, and were often also united by ties of blood. Geoffrey Robinson writes that 'practically all the farmers and master-craftsmen at Hedingham were closely enough related to my grand-father (the blacksmith) to be regarded as his cousins.'

One actual cousin, Charlie Rudkin, was the village bootmaker, a self-educated man who also acted as a legal advisor in village prob-lems, and eventually became a magistrate. He was, in fact, the archetypal village shoemaker, 'a lawyer in all but qualification, a scholar in all but formal education, and the wise man of the village.'

The work of such craftsmen was essential to the fabric of village life. As Walter Rose writes in *The Village Carpenter:*

> The work that we executed was closely related to the life of the village, and of the district for a few miles round. There was continual going and coming from the shop to the places for which the work was intended; a few days' work in the shop, making doors, windows or other fitments for a house or farm, then a period at the place fixing the work, and doing what else was required there. Thus we were ever in contact with the life of the village, and a necessary part of its communal existence.

Rose stresses the craftsmen's pride in their work, and in their tools, which they treated reverently and guarded possessively. The same sense of pride in craft is very strong in George Sturt's account of his family's wheelwright's shop. He remarks how, when he took over the shop, the men kept rigidly to their own high standards, refusing in disgust to use any materials which they thought inferior. 'In this temper,' he writes, 'the shop, I feel sure, turned out good work.' One particular workman typified the virtues of all:

> Especially the wheels which George Cook used to make were, I am bound to think, as good as any that had been built under the eyes of two

57

experts like my father and his father. Cook, it is pretty sure, took his own time; but what a workman he was! There was another wheel-wright in the shop whose wife used to take out garden produce in a little van: and when the van wanted new wheels, this man would not make them himself but asked that George Cook might make them. Truly, it was a liberal education to work under Cook's guidance. I never could get axe or plane or chisel sharp enough to satisfy him; but I never doubted, then or since, that his tiresome fastidiousness over tools and handiwork sprang from a knowledge as valid as any artist's. He knew, not by theory, but more delicately, in his eyes and fingers. Yet there were others almost his match – men who could make the wheels, and saw out on the saw-pit the other timbers for a dung-cart, and build the cart and paint it – preparing the paint first; or, if need be, help the blacksmith tyring the wheels.

This level of accomplishment was the rule in village craftsmen, but in a less obvious way it was true too for the farm labourer. The labourers, like the craftsmen, preserved and served a local and tradi-tional lore and knowledge which turned their work, in their own minds, from unskilled wage labour into an 'art, craft and mystery'. The sense of heritage, of something handed down from one genera-tion to the next, something which had nothing to do with legal ownership of land, was palpable. It is still to be felt in, for instance, Flora Thompson's restrained and modest picture of ploughmen at work:

> There were usually three or four ploughs to a field, each of them drawn by a team of three horses, with a boy at the head of the leader and the ploughman behind at the shafts. All day, up and down they would go ribbing the pale stubble with stripes of dark furrows, which, as the day advanced, would get wider and nearer together, until, at length. the whole field lay a rich velvety plum-colour
> Each plough had its following of rooks, searching the clods with sidelong glances for worms and grubs. Little hedgerow birds flitted hither and thither, intent upon getting their tiny share of whatever was going. Sheep, penned in a neighbouring field, bleated complainingly; and above the ma-a-ing and cawing and twittering rose the immemor-ial cries of the landworker: 'Wert up!' 'Who-o-o-a!' 'Go it, Poppet!' 'Go it, Lightfoot!' 'Boo-oy, be you deaf, or be you hard of hearin', dang ye!'

4

O MOTHER I LONGS TO GET MARRIED

ᴇ§ SEX AND MARRIAGE §ᴇ

O mother I longs to get married
I longs to be a bride.
I longs to lay by that young man,
And close to by his side.
Close to by his side,
O happy I should be,
For I'm young and merry
And almost weary
Of my virginity.

FOLK SONG

THE RITUALS OF courtship in the English village were open to
misunderstanding from outside the community. Not least of these
was the widespread practice of delaying marriage until the girl was
pregnant. Seen by middle-class moralists as evidence of 'immorality',
for the country workfolk it represented a morality based on practica-
lity, relieving young couples of the hardships of setting up home for
as long as possible, and also confirming the woman's child-bearing
ability. A reporter in the *Morning Chronicle* in 1850 writes, 'It really
seems, in many places, to be taken as a matter of course that a young
woman will be found with child before she is married. Many are
married as soon as they become pregnant.'

It is certainly true that cottage girls had little chance to preserve the
maidenly modesty that was the Victorian ideal. Overcrowding in
cottages was commonly held by obervers to encourage sexual irregu-
larity, especially incest, and to be one of the causes of the drift of
country girls into prostitution: according to the *Saturday Review* in
1858, 'the cottage bedroom was the first stop to the Haymarket.' It is

impossible now to disentangle the prejudices of the commentators from the evidence they present, but their overheated language reveals a limited understanding of the problems of families living in cramped and inadequate conditions, 'great boys and girls, mothers and fathers, all sleeping in one room in many instances.' While modern experience has revealed that incest is more frequent at all levels of society than anyone cares to admit, there are no reasons for regarding it as especially rife among nineteenth-century villagers.

Another fear of the moralists was that outdoor work would irretrievably coarsen girls, and unfit them for 'a woman's proper duties at home'. In her discussion of this question in her admirable essay 'Country Work Girls', Jennie Kitteringham quotes Dr Julian Hunter, writing in 1864:

> That which seems most to lower the moral or decent tone of the peasant girls is the sensation of independence of society which they acquire when they have remunerative labour in their hands either in the fields, or at home as strawplaiters, etc. All gregarious employment gives a slang character to the girls' appearance and habits, while dependence on the man for support is the spring of modest and pleasing behaviour.

One of the reasons why worried clergymen got so worked up about the 'immorality' of country girls is that they, like Dr Hunter, subscribed to this view of the ideal relations between man and woman, a view which was not at all echoed in the culture of the workfolk, whose harsher experience of life demanded a more equal contribution from both sexes. As George Sturt noted in *Change in the Village*:

> The main fact is that the two sexes, each engaged daily upon essential duties, stand on a surprising equality the one to the other. And where the men are so well aware of the women's experienced outlook, and the women so well aware of the men's, the affectation of ignorance might almost be construed as a form of immodesty, or at any rate as an impudence. It would, indeed, be too absurd to pretend that these wives and mothers, who have to face every trial of life and death for themselves, do not know the things which obviously they cannot help knowing; too absurd to treat them as though they were all innocence, timidity, and daintiness. No labouring man would esteem a woman for delicacy of that kind, and the women certainly would not like to be esteemed for it. Hence the sexes habitually meet on almost level terms.

It was common, for instance, for men to hand over their wages unopened to their wives, and for women to have complete control over the family finances. Nevertheless there is force in Sturt's qualification, 'almost level terms'. The farmworker James Bowd wrote a brief memoir in 1889, at the age of 66, in which he writes very tenderly of his early married years. 'I was as fond of my wife,' he says, 'Has a Cat is of New Milk.' But 'I felt as if I Dare not tell her how much I Loved her because I thought she Would be trespising on were I should be and that would be the Head of the house.'

Some of the clearest evidence of sexual attitudes and sexual behaviour is contained not in memoirs, which are usually reticent about such matters, nor in official reports, which are class-biased, but in the earthy symbolism of folk song. English folk songs reveal, in what James Reeves has happily called 'the idiom of the people', a suprisingly open sexuality quite removed from the coyness of the Victorian middle classes. From the girl who insists on playing 'all fours' to the cobbler proud of his 'long pegging-awl', the corpus of English folksong is full of erotic encounters, many initiated by the woman, and almost all occasions of mutual enjoyment. The folk attitude is well expressed in the song 'Hares on the Mountains', recorded in this version by H.E.D. Hammond from John Seaward at Charmouth, April 1906:

> If young women were ducks, they'd swim on the water.
> All the young men would strip and swim after.
>
> If young women were hares, they'd run on the mountain.
> All the young men would soon ride a-hunting.
>
> If young women were lambs, they'd lie on the common.
> All the young men would lie alongside on 'em.

We know from many accounts that there was a good deal of bawdy banter and play in the fields, especially during haymaking, and that the hiring-fairs known as statute or mop fairs were also occasions of licensed indulgence, but much of this behaviour expressed a sense of simple fun rather than unusual sexual freedom. While some country girls were no doubt promiscuous, and as we have seen those who took up cottage industries such as lace-making, straw plait and gloving were often regarded as little more than prostitutes, the Victorian ideals of chastity and fidelity were strongly reflected among the rural poor as in the rest of society.

Girls nourished romantic dreams of their future husbands, and employed many traditional means to discover who they were to marry. One of the most popular was divination by means of a Bible and key. The folklorist Sidney Oldall Addy gives the following instructions:

> Take a Bible, tie it round with your garter... and twirl it round with a key inserted in the loop, repeating Ruth's adjuration, 'Entreat me not to leave thee,' etc., the while. Then untwirl it, and, as you do so, repeat the letters of the alphabet. The letters which come next before the stopping of the twirling will be the initial letters sought for.

Similarly,

> if a girl wishes to dream of her future husband let her go upstairs backwards on a Tuesday or Friday night with a garter in her hands, saying these words as she ties it:
> > I tie my garter in two knots
> > That I my beloved may see,
> > Not in his best apparel,
> > But in the clothes he wears every day.

The wish to see the young man in his everyday clothes, which recurs in many such formulae, shows that the girls were not dreaming of rising out of their station: the sweetheart they were summoning was one of their own class. Their hearts were set on a 'bonny labouring boy' like the one in the folk song:

> Oh his cheeks are like the roses, his eyes so black as sloes,
> He smiles in his behaviour wherever my love goes.
> He's manly, neat and handsome, his skin so white as snow,
> In spite of all my parents with my labouring boy I'll go.

Rural courtship was not necessarily the rough, coarse affair one might imagine. Just as the girls cherished romantic dreams, so too the young men struggled to express their deeper longings. George Baldry's modesty and reticence are familiar from other accounts. He paid little attention to girls:

> Till one afternoon when with the other boys I were a-running up the school yard fit to bust ourselves, to see who could git to the end first, I see a girl going past the school gate, hand-in-hand with a young sister of hers. I was so struck I fell in love there and then, the first time I had ever known what it meant.

Such a change had come over me, young as I was, that she was always in my mind's eye, and very often if I knew she was out for a walk or on an errand I would go round another way so that I might meet her and git her to smile. Many and many a time have I done that. I was very shy at the time with girls, and it was many a day before I plucked up the heart to speak to her. The amusing part of it was, as I have thought since, I was courting her in my boyish way hoping she would some day be my wife, as come to pass in the end after many a long year, when we was neither of us young no longer. She not knowing anything about it gave me no encouragement which but strengthened my love, and I was only a kid – just out of the cradle – dare not tell anyone. I kept it quiet for years and waited my time.

This long steadfastness was not unusual; nor was the sense of love at first sight. Love, a lifetime's bonding heart and soul, was the aim of both sexes.

There were local problems. In villages where all the girls went out to service in their early teens, there might be a shortage of brides, and records show that husband and wife did often come from different villages. But the basic dream of finding one's mate and settling down for life seems to have been as strong among the labouring classes as it was among the wealthy, whose appetite for matchmaking is well displayed in the diaries of the Gloucestershire squire Dearman Birchall.

Village girls were not, of course, brought up in the protective cocoon of their middle and upper class counterparts. Their very rhymes, such as this one recorded in Hanging Heaton in Yorskshire but known in variations throughout the country, show a keen awareness of sexual matters:

Mary mixed a pudding up,
She mixed it very sweet,
She daren't stick a knife in
Till John came home at neet.
Taste John, taste John, don't say nay,
Perhaps tomorrow morning will be our wedding-day.

Richard Jefferies describes how 'sometimes three or four together, joining hands, dance slowly round and round, singing slowly rude rhymes describing marriage – and not over decent some of these rhymes are.' It was probably such behaviour – which he may have interpreted as provocative – which led Francis Kilvert, rector of

Langley Burrell, Wilts, to find himself on 16 February 1874 'Greatly troubled by the licentiousness of the school children, especially Harriet Ferris, Mary Grimshaw and Lucy Halliday.'

There was no way that such girls, however innocent, could remain ignorant. As Jefferies writes:

> The overcrowding in cottages leads to what may be called an indifference to decency. It is not that in families decency is wantonly and of a set purpose disregarded, but stern necessity leads to a coarseness and indelicacy which hardens the mind and deadens the natural modesty of even the best girls. Then the low scandals of the village talked over from cottage to cottage, the rude jokes of the hayfield, the general looseness and indifference which prevail as to morality, all prepare the girl for the too common fall.

According to another country parson, Augustus Jessopp, 'in the best of times chastity never was a virtue held in very high estimation among the rural population.' Abortion was little known, though some herbs, such as pennyroyal, were prized as abortifacients. In *My Secret Life*, Walter reports that when Martha, a cottage girl whom he paid for sex, fell pregnant (got 'poisoned', in the local parlance), her sister 'took Martha to a fortune-teller, and she got better of her difficulty.' Presumably by 'fortune-teller' he means wise woman or 'cunning man'. It does not sound as if this was a physically procured abortion; she must have been dosed with some noxious preparation. At a time when contraception was virtually unknown, the only possible precaution was to practice *coitus interruptus* or 'pullback', but this was as unreliable as it was unsatisfying. The result was that, as W.H. Hudson reported from Sussex, 'In some of the villages illegitimate children are as plentiful as blackberries.'

Within marriage, large families were inevitable. Flora Thompson records an attitude of scorn towards those who admitted using *coitus interruptus* in marriage, though she also notes a bitter female proverb: 'The wife ought to have the first child and the husband the second, then there wouldn't ever be any more.' The high rate of infant mortality, while a source of terrible grief to many, was necessary if families were to survive. In some areas, notably the fens, the frequent death of babies from semi-starvation and overdosing with opiates amounted to infanticide by deliberate neglect.

If children both arrived and died too easily, sex was still a strong pull. Richard Jefferies overheard what is surely a traditional saying in a cottage wife's reply to the busybody who rebuked her 'for having that fifteenth boy': 'Lor, miss, that's all the pleasure me an' my old man got.'

Large families and overcrowded homes were one incentive to early marriages. As Jefferies again tells us, 'The cottage girls and cottage boys marry the instant they get a chance, and it is not at all uncommon to find comparatively young labourers who have had two wives.' The more prudent, such as Isaac Mead, put off marriage till they had some money saved. Isaac and his sweetheart were engaged for five years, determined 'We should not get married time I was a journeyman.' But such self-restraint and inner purpose could only be the exception, not the rule. Jefferies' *Note-Books* for 1883 condense his conversation with a cottage woman into the laconic line, 'Married before she knew the difference between one man and another.'

Marriage itself under these conditions was often, as a comic dialogue popular in Wiltshire put it, a 'Struggle for the Breeches'. The need to make ends meet under almost impossible conditions – as well, no doubt, as the stress caused by the desire for sexual relations hampered by the fear of conception – led to many clashes of will and personality. Again according to Jefferies, 'The attachment of the woman for her husband lasts longer than that of the man for the woman.'

Some of the strains of marriage in this class of society emerge in the anonymous 'Autobiography of a Navvy', whose author was an agricultural labourer who went 'on tramp' in the hungry '40s and married Anne, a straw plaiter, in Baldock, Herts, around 1850. He determined to marry her even though he had only spoken to her once in passing. He writes:

> When first I married I used to sit and look at my wife plaiting till the blood ran out at the ends of her fingers; and when she'd done a good bit I'd say, 'Now, old gal, go and sell that plait and get me a pint of beer.'

J. Millott Severn anatomises his own parents' unhappy marriage in his autobiography. They were an ill-matched pair, 'Constant disagreements prevailed, nothing seemed to reconcile them.' After the death of a baby girl, when Joseph was three, 'my mother decided to go away and leave everything, and earn her own living. My sister Emmey, a few years older than myself, was packed off to Derby, to be with one of our aunts, and I was left with father.' In the week, he lived with his uncle and aunt and grandfather. His mother took a situation as a nurse with a well-to-do family; after a few years she returned home, and soon another boy was born. This pattern of separation and return is a familiar one, though it was usually the husband who left.

Severn's parents marriage is interesting in another way, in that it reveals what was again a fairly frequent method of finding a partner. His father had been happily married to a consumptive who 'realising that her end was near, was so concerned regarding father's happiness, that she sent for a late companion of hers, with whom she had lived as a fellow servant, and got her to promise that she would marry father if he so wished, after her decease. That companion was my mother.' His mother had been previously engaged, but the liaison was broken off by the boy's parents on class grounds.

It would be a mistake, however, to suppose that most marriages were as troubled as this. While most autobiographers are as silent about their deeper emotional life as about their sexual life, many bear witness to the sustaining comradeship which is one of the chief pleasures of marriage. One thinks, for instance, of the Sussex singer and bell-ringer Henry Burstow celebrating his wife's 78th birthday by singing her his entire repertoire of 420 songs:

> I sang about ten on 41 consecutive evenings, and as we sat, evening after evening, one on either side of the fire, as happy as a king and queen, I singing my best, she listening and occasionally herself singing one of the fifty songs I had taught her, the old songs seemed as fresh and pretty as they did when I first sang them fifty, sixty, perhaps seventy years or more ago.

The unnamed 'King of the Norfolk Poachers' records the loss of his wife in childbirth with moving economy:

> The days went on till the time come for her confinement, wen to my great sorrow she died. Young as I was then it was the hardest blow I have ever had to bear in all my life, the more so because it came so sudden, and there was no reason I knew it should all end like that, and no warning. She did not want to go and I had lost a dear pall as well as a loven wife, and she had left me with a new born baby – for the child, a boy, lived.

Joseph Ashby had a conversation with an aged Primitive Methodist labourer who was worried that the vicar would not allow him to be buried in the old section of the churchyard where his wife was buried:

'I wants to be laad wi' my old 'ooman. Us ought to waake up together.... I thinks of 'er lookin' for me, all in a confusion, bothered because I ent theer.'

It is true, however, that this ideal of lifelong companionship and support co-existed with more casual attitudes, and that behaviour which would have brought shame on the educated classes was cheerfully accepted among the uneducated. While it was still illegal, for instance, it was common, especially among dissenters, for men to marry their deceased wife's sister. Augustus Jessopp describes one unconventional Norfolk couple, whose story he insists is 'simple truth':

> It is as little reproach to Dick Styles that he has been three times in gaol as it was in Dick's eyes that Polly Beck had had five children in a miscellaneous kind of way when he married her. Dick is an habitual drunkard; his first wife died and left him with two children, the eldest three years old. Dick had so bad a character that no one would be his housekeeper; the neighbours 'did for' the poor children. In ten days Dick's patience was exhausted. Off he walked to the union workhouse, got admission on some pretext to the women's ward, and gave out that he wanted a wife and wouldn't go till he had got one. An eager crowd of females offered themselves. He picked out the prettiest. 'What's your name?' 'Polly Beck.' 'How many children?' 'Three!' 'Who's the father?' 'Don't know! I had two by Jack the butcher, they died, and he took up with a Norman – many blessings on her! T'other three ain't so very big.' In less than an hour Dick, Polly, and the three little ones marched out together happily. At the registrar's office, within a month, Polly became Mrs Styles, and turned out not such a bad wife. For Dick was *only* a drunkard, and she was an audacious, high-spirited little woman, who, with all her faults, had a knack of making the best of a bad bargain.

Women such as Polly provided one outlet for a village's sexual tensions in casual prostitution. The vast army of Victorian prostitutes, including many country girls, flocked to the large towns, but as Jessopp noted, 'female prostitution in country villages is by no means uncommon.' Women widowed or abandoned by their husbands had a hard time keeping afloat, and there must have been many scenes such as that in Richard Jefferies' 'A True Tale of the Wiltshire Labourer', in which the deserted wife, Madge, is approached by the farmer:

He put his hand on her shoulder and muttered something in her ear. Madge seemed scarcely to understand him, but sat staring wildly.

'I'll give thee sixpence,' said Humphreys, showing one.

Sexual safety valves such as this might well earn a community's tacit sanction. What was not acceptable was the adulterous affair, which struck at the roots of the village's social organisation. Sturt notes the 'remarkable fidelity' of married couples. Where infidelity was suspected, village communities throughout England resorted to 'rough music' to show their displeasure. Known under various names as 'skimmington', 'riding the stang', 'ran-tanning' and so on, this widespread custom is mentioned in many memoirs. The whole village gathered outside the miscreant's house with pots, pans and scrap metal which were beaten to make the cacophonous 'rough music'. Effigies of the offenders might be exhibited and even burnt, and harsh criticisms delivered in traditional verse. This exhibition sometimes continued over three nights, and those at the receiving end either mended their ways or left the village. The custom was made an offence against the Highway Act of 1882, but continued sporadically after that date. Readers will recall the 'skimmity-ride' in Hardy's *Mayor of Casterbridge*.

Rough music was also used in severe cases of wife-beating. The chants used are hypnotic, minatory:

> With a ran, dan, dan,
> Sing o' my owd frying-pan
> A brazen-faced villain has been paying his best woman:
> He neither paid her wi' stick, stake, nor a stower,
> But he up wi' his fisses an he knocked her ower.

Jefferies writes:

> Although serious wife-beating cases are infrequent, there are few women who escape an occasional blow from their husbands. Most of them get a moderate amount of thrashing in the course of their lives, and take it as much as they take the hardships and poverty of their condition, as a necessity not to be escaped. The labourer is not downright brutal to his wife, but he certainly thinks he has a right to chastise her when she displeases him.

Jefferies' story 'John Smith's Shanty', written in 1874, gives us the man's side of such a case, in the words of a good man driven to violence by desperation:

She asked I for money, she did, and what was I to gi'e her? I hadn't got a shilling nor a sixpence, and she knew it, and knowed that I couldn't get one either till Saturday night. I gets thirteen shillings a week from Master H., and a shilling on Sundays, and I hev got five children and a wife to keep out of that – that's two shillings a week for each on us, that's just threepence halfpenny a day, look 'ee, sir. And what victuals be I to buy wi' that, let alone beer? and a man can't do no work wi'out a quart a day, and that's fourpence, and there's my share, look 'ee, gone at onst. Wur be I to get any victuals, and wur be I to get any clothes and boots, I should like for to know? And Jack he gets big and wants a main lot, and so did Polly, but her's gone to the work'us, wuss luck. And parson wants I to send the young 'uns to school, and pay a penny a week for 'em, and missis she wants a bit o' bacon in the house and a loaf, and what good is that of, among all we? I gets a slice of bacon twice a week, and sometimes narn. And beer – I knows I drinks beer, and more as I ought, but what's a chap to do when he's a'most shrammed wi' cold, and nar a bit o' nothin' in the pot but an old yeller swede as hard as wood? And my teeth bean't as good as 'em used to be. I knows I drinks beer, and so would anybody in my place – it makes me kinder stupid, as I don't feel nothing then. Wot's the good – I've worked this thirty year or more, since I wur big enough to go with the plough, and I've a knowed they as have worked for nigh handy sixty, and wot do 'em get for it? All he'd a got wur the rheumatiz. Yer med as well drink wile 'ee can. I never meaned to hurt her, and her knows it; and if it wurn't for a parcel of women a-shoving on her on, her would never a come here agen me. I knows I drinks, and what else be I to do? I can't work allus.

Apart from desertion by one partner or the other, there was no way out of an unhappy marriage. Wife-selling as a form of popular divorce, while still occurring sporadically in the nineteenth century, surviving most strongly in the industrialized north, particularly Yorkshire, was already an obscure and almost unbelievable custom when *The Mayor of Casterbridge* was published in 1886, while despite the Divorce Act of 1857 legal divorce would not be a real option for the masses for many years to come.

A stray jotting in Jefferies' *Note-Books*, while it may simply be the idea for a story, hints at a less formalised level of rural wife-swapping: 'Barter of wives. "I be tired of mine: let's have your-n a bit. Ar-right." In Pothouse.' A recently-unearthed note made by C.Y. Bickley towards the end of the century and printed in *FLS News*, 17 June 1993, suggests that at least in some villages, such customs were not unknown:

> Woking village, Surrey. It has been a custom in this village for the lower stratum of the male inhabitants to meet at a public house, and (informally) arrange for an exchange of wives. No fixed period of cohabitation was agreed on, but it appears to have been limited to one night. On separating the men proceeded to the house of the allotted woman. As the women never objected, and no questions of paternity were raised, the habit would appear to be customary; and, ten years ago, the earliest instance of which I have knowledge, the arrangement was spoken of as a matter of course. I have not heard anything to lead to any date of origin, nor did the affair appear to be deemed immoral. There are no records of the custom but possibly a research in the diocesan archives might reveal the raising of questions of discipline.

Some chose to remain unmarried. No doubt some were homosexual in inclination, while others were victims of lack of chance or choice. But others still were cynical about the whole business, like the old Northumbrian who was asked in 1871 by Richard Heath why he had never married:

> Because a woman in Northumberland's not worth house-room. Why, you see, sir, she's out in the field all day, and knows nothing about housework. A man can do varra superior to the vast of them.

5

PITY POOR LABOURERS

ᘀᔒ THE STANDARD OF LIVING ᔒᘀ

O, the poor labourers, pity poor labourers,
That are working for five or six shillings per week.
TRADITIONAL

THE BULK OF the rural population was very poor. Their average weekly cash wage in 1851 was nine shillings and seven pence, though this was augmented by various perquisites. Most workers could have echoed the labourer who forlornly told Alexander Somerville 'It ben't easy out of our income to get a bellyful for so many.'

One of the results, as we have seen, is that children were sent out to work at an early age, and mothers had to neglect their families to toil for minimal additions to the family wage. Even so, wives had to be expert at managing the income if their families were not to face ruin and starvation. Flora Thompson writes:

> Many husbands boasted that they never asked their wives what they did with the money. As long as there was food enough, clothes to cover everybody, and a roof over their heads, they were satisfied, they said, and they seemed to make a virtue of this and think what generous, trusting, fine-hearted fellows they were. If a wife got into debt or complained, she was told: 'You must larn to cut your coat accordin' to your cloth, my gal.' The coats not only needed expert cutting, but should have been made of elastic.

Something of the vicissitudes of such a life comes through in the interrogation of a Bucks labourer named Pitkin by the 1895 Royal Commission on the Aged Poor, which included Lord Aberdare and the Prince of Wales as well as Joseph Arch, the agricultural labourers' leader who was by then a Member of Parliament. Pitkin had worked for forty years, commencing at eight shillings a week; his wage was then thirteen shillings:

> It used to rise and sink very often, according as the markets were. Sometimes we would get eight shillings in the winter and nine shillings in the spring time . . . but the wages have always been better since the railway was cut through our place; they began to rise.

This pattern occured throughout the country. For instance when in 1873 the railway was being built from Watchet to Minehead in Somerset, paying 3s 3d a day or about £1 a week, this did raise wages, but not above 11s a week, plus an allowance of two pints of cider a day. This cider was valued at 2s a week, but overvalued, especially as the men were usually given the much inferior second-pressing cider rather than the good quality first pressing kept for the farmer's own use.

Pitkin's worst period was when his wife fell ill, and for six years 'could not walk without being led': 'I do not know how I did get on. I was nearly starved.' The Prince of Wales asked him whether he had been able to save anything as a young man:

> No, I was not. My wife was very ill, and I had a large family, and I could hardly get food, and it took me a long time before I could save a pound – a long time it did. My wife was so ill, and altogether that pulled me right down to the thread.

While, before the agricultural depression, the middle and upper class villagers shared in the prosperity of the times, the majority lived from hand to mouth, like the Norfolk family described by Augustus Jessopp, 'living and dying in a squalid hovel with a clay floor and two dark cabins under the rafters, reached by a rickety ladder; in the one of which sleep father and mother as best they can, while in the foetid air of the other their offspring of both sexes huddle, sometimes eight or nine of them, among them young men and young women out of whom you are stamping all sense of shame.'

Cottages, of course, varied from estate to estate, village to village, region to region, both in their state of repair and in their architectural style. Like all vernacular architecture, the construction of the village home was largely determined by the local materials available, as Richard Heath points out:

> With their gable roofs of cosy thatch or of red tiles bright with moss and lichen, with their ornamented chimneys and walls of plaster laced

and interlaced with heavy beams, the Cottage Homes of England, peeping out from the green lanes of Kent, or fringing the Surrey commons, or nestling in the wooded vales of Sussex, are always picturesque. They are, moreover, the one form of human habitation always in harmony with the scenery around them. In Yorkshire and in Wales their aspect is bleak as the moor or the mountain side; in Cumberland and in Devonshire they are alike built of stone; but in the north their architecture is in keeping with the stern form Nature presents among the Cumbrian hills; while in the south, covered with ivy and hidden amongst gardens and orchards, each little cot appears a poem in itself. This harmony is partly due to the fact that the same soil which produces the natural scenery produces the material of which the cottages are built. In the north wood is scarce, stone plentiful: hence the stone villages of Lancashire and Yorkshire. In the pottery districts and the midland counties clay is abundant; here, therefore, brick cottages are the rule. In Westmorland the red sandstone is used; in Kent the ragstone, in Lincolnshire the Ancaster stone, in Cornwall granite, in Essex and Herts flints from the chalk hills, in Hampshire mud mixed with pebbles, in Norfolk and Suffolk lumps of clay mixed with straw.

In all these landscapes, one thing was constant. If you looked behind the picturesque, cosy exterior, 'you will find', writes George Francis Millin, 'it is a filthy, dilapidated pig-sty of a place, in a condition utterly unfit for human habitation.'

Some squires and farmers did spend considerable sums erecting model cottages which offered a very poor return on outlay, but generally speaking village housing was dilapidated and inapropriate. Francis George Heath's 1874 account of cottages in the village of Montacute, Somerset, the seat of the Phelips family, can stand for many:

> The one bedroom over the stone floor apartment was a kind of attic, almost entirely denuded of furniture. There was a window on each side. But several panes of the glass had been broken, and the holes stuffed with rags. In this one small wretched apartment, in some parts of which I could not have stood upright, the eight persons composing this family had to sleep – father, mother, and six children. The mother told me that at one time the family living at home consisted of no less than thirteen persons, who all had to sleep in the one small bedroom of the cottage.

The cottages of Montacute were generally distinguished by their 'chilling air of misery and wretchedness', and yet 'this village was renowned for the prosperity of its farmers, the land in the district being some of the richest in the whole country.'

To be fair to landlords, some of the very worst houses were 'mushroom' hovels thrown up on waste land by the cottagers themselves; these were, according to the Rev. J. Fraser in Norfolk, 'wretched dens'.

Inside such cramped, dark and insanitary homes, the cottage wives brought up their large families. Inevitable, cooking was of the simplest kind. Where there was no oven or range, food was mostly boiled at fireplaces fitted with open grates or with hooks from which a cooking pot or boiler could be suspended. Some cottages had bread ovens, but often there were communal bakehouses for rows of cottages, in which hot meals could be baked in the residual heat after bread-baking, notably for Sunday dinner.

The fire for cooking was fed with coal, coke, wood, furze, and household refuse (including vegetable peelings where no pig was kept). Finding fuel – except in mining districts where coal was cheap – was a constant worry, and the availability and cost of fuel was a major factor in diet: less hot food was prepared in southern England where fuel was scarce and expensive.

While the labourer's diet varied in different areas, it was always very simple. Salted pork, with swede or turnip tops, potatoes and bread formed staples; there was always a sharp distinction between pork and 'butcher's meat'. In addition, many villagers caught and ate sparrows and other garden birds.

Edwin Grey describes the favoured luncheon for male workers at Harpenden, Herts, as 'bread and cheese, a raw onion, together with a pint of beer, "a meal fit fer a King ter ev." I've heard men remark.' This is, of course, the origin of the 'ploughman's lunch' which is still popular pub fare. Cold tea was an alternative to beer, and the men also heated meals on outdoor fires, grilling bloaters with improvised toasting forks. Meat dumplings made of potato, onion, parsley and finely chopped poor cuts of meat were also popular.

Bread, potatoes and tea were the mainstays, supplemented with sugar and treacle; bacon in better times; butcher's meat a luxury. There were fewer local variations in this impoverished diet than might be expected. There were various unleavened flour-and-water mixtures such as the mournfully titled 'sad cakes' and the scarcely edible 'Sussex pudding'; in the West of England there were Cornish pasties; in the north there were oatmeal or barley bannocks, and pease pudding. An old Northumbrian, William Stenhouse of Wark, waxed warm to Arthur Fox in 1893 about the perils of abandoning this traditional diet:

> A man should eat the food of the country in which he is born. This foreign stuff, such as tea, is no forage for a man. Bannocks made of barley and peas made a man as hard as a brick. Men would take a lump of bannock out for the day, and drink water, but now they eat white bread and drink tea, and ain't half so hard.

Richard Jefferies gives a fair picture of the usual diet:

> Their food is of the rudest and scantiest, chiefly weak tea, without milk, sweetened with moist sugar, and hunches of dry bread, sometimes with a little lard, or, for a treat, with treacle. Butter is scarcely ever used in the agricultural labourer's cottage. It is too dear by far, and if he does buy fats, he believes in the fats expressed from meats, and prefers lard or dripping. Children are frequently fed with bread and cheap sugar spread on it. This is much cheaper than butter. Sometimes they get a bit of cheese or bacon, but not often, and a good deal of strong cabbage, soddened with pot-liquor. The elder boys get a little beer; the young girls none, save perhaps a sip from their mother's pint, in summer. This is what they have to build up a frame on capable of sustaining heat and cold, exposure, and a life of endless labour.

Elsewhere, Jefferies is critical of this unimaginative cuisine, comparing it with the rich peasant fare of the continent, but the truth was that most of the rural workforce had not so much as a piece of ground to till for themselves. Allotments, when available, might be a couple of miles from home, but even so they were much prized, and those lucky enough to have a vegetable garden or allotment, or somewhere to keep a pig, were considerably better off. Jefferies describes such gardens in terms which show how proudly they were kept:

> Trees fill up every available space and corner – apple trees, pear trees, damsons, plums, bullaces – all varieties. The cottagers seem to like to have at least one tree of every sort. These trees look very nice in the spring when the apple blossom is out, and again in the autumn when the fruit is ripe. Under the trees are gooseberry bushes, raspberries, and numbers of currants. The patches are divided into strips producing potatoes, cabbage, lettuce, onions, radishes, parsnips; in this kitchen produce, as with the fruit, they like to possess a few of all kinds. There is generally a great bunch of rhubarb.

Generally speaking the poor without gardens or allotments had to buy their food, either with ready money or on tick. The quality of this fare was often poor. There was deliberate adulteration either by shopkeepers or by dealers, and there was a risk of contamination because of insanitary storage. Both of these matters were a further threat to the cottagers' constitutions. Bread was adulterated with alum and potato; flour with chalk; beer with sulphate of iron; spent tea-leaves were re-dyed with various substances and re-sold; tea leaves were mixed with hedgerow clippings; milk was watered, where it was even available: ironically, fresh milk was hard to come by in many rural districts. Because public institutions such as workhouses were supplied by tender, the quality of the food was often very low, although even so it might be better and more varied than that which the inmates were used to.

Payment in kind (the 'truck' system) was widespread, and often obliged the workers to buy inferior goods at inflated prices. 'Truck' could be a way for farmers to sell goods – such as the meat from diseased animals – which could never find a competitive market. For instance the 'grist' corn which Somerset workers could buy at a special price, and which was regarded as a great privilege, was actually the rakings from the field after the bulk of the crop had been harvested, and had often begun to sprout through lying in the wet, thus rendering it unsaleable elsewhere. On the other hand, corn gleaned by the cottagers themselves from the harvest fields made a considerable contribution to the household economy.

Those cottagers who were able to keep a pig prized this highly. Often a pig would be used as a surety for credit with village tradesmen; Flora Thompson recalled that 'half a pig' would be mortgaged to the baker or miller, while the other half would provide the family with bacon. Pig-killing was a dramatic, ritual affair, as she recalls it from her childhood at Juniper Hill:

> The next thing was to engage the travelling pork butcher, or pig-sticker, and, as he was a thatcher by day, he always had to kill after dark, the scene being lighted with lanterns and the fire of burning straw which at a later stage of the proceedings was to singe the bristles off the victim.
>
> The killing was a noisy, bloody business, in the course of which the animal was hoisted to a rough bench that it might bleed thoroughly and so preserve the quality of the meat. The job was often bungled, the pig

sometimes getting away and having to be chased; but country people of that day had little sympathy for the sufferings of animals, and men, women, and children would gather round to see the sight.

On the other hand, many villagers kept pets; Joseph Ashby's uncle, for instance, had a pet badger.

Village shops, often run by women, kept a small, varied stock of life's necessities. Richard Jefferies recalled the village shop of his home village of Coate as 'a shop window about two feet square: snuff and tobacco, bread and cheese, immense big round jumbles and sugar, kept on the floor above and reached down by hand, when wanted, through the opening for the ladder stairs.' As shops took over more of the business of the itinerant hawkers of an earlier day, and especially once the creation of a national postal service required the setting up of a system of sub-post offices, these tiny village shops either expanded to meet demand or disappeared in the face of competition from nearby towns.

Clothing would generally be purchased from the nearest town except in larger villages which might have one or two draper's shops. In addition, packmen would call from town and take orders for clothing to be paid for in weekly instalments. As the century wore on, the time-honoured outfits of the villagers were modified by the availability of cheap ready-made clothes and also by a new awareness in both women and men of contemporary fashion, through the circulation of illustrated magazines. In particular the old labourer's smock frock fell into disuse.

Edwin Grey describes the Hertfordshire labourers' attire in the 1870s as follows: a 'wideawake' hat, the brim of which could be turned down all round as a shield against sun or rain (and possibly a hand-me-down top hat for Sunday best); smocks, being replaced by 'slop' canvas jackets; short thick 'Reefer' overcoats of black or navy; corduroy trousers with or without leather leggings; a neck hand-kerchief; white cotton stockings, often with the feet cut off and replaced by wrappings of white linen, and good boots, often with a lining of hay. While young children might run around barefoot, stout boots were crucial for anyone working on the land, and were a considerable expense for most families. Consequently they were treated with great care:

All wore thick, stout-soled boots, well studded with nails and tipped heel and toe, often also keeping a lighter pair less heavily nailed, or may be unnailed, for specials. The boots were frequently examined and any missing nails or tips replaced. Nearly every cottage possessed a hobbling foot for use in these repairing jobs, and also in most cottages a grease pot was kept, wherein odds and ends of tallow candles were deposited for use in winter time; in snowy weather boots were given a good dressing of the hot grease, this to keep out the penetrating snow water, and at the same time keeping the leather in pliable condition.

The younger men might also possess a ready-made cloth suit for best, often bought for their wedding day.

Women's wear was generally either a plain skirt with a bodice frock or a print dress, with layers of flannel petticoats, and wooden pattens to protect shoes and stockings in the mud; older women still wore white aprons and modified crinolines, and old-fashioned bonnets. In the 1860s and 70s, J. Millott Severn's mother in Codnor, near Matlock, added considerably to the family income by dressmaking, and in particular making crinolines, which he remembered as worn by 'quite poor people, and young women as well as old'. She also purchased a treadle sewing machine by instalments and 'soon began to do a nice bit of business in machine sewing for the village folk, doing seams and straight runs at three yards a penny.'

Clothes were washed by boiling them up in large iron boilers and by scrubbing them in wooden troughs. Houses had no sinks, and, of course, no electricity or running water. Water was either collected in rain barrels or brought from wells: difficult, heavy work.

Most cottages had cesspool closets, 'privies', shared between up to six cottages, and emptied at night, the men taking turns for this disagreeable job. The night soil was used on gardens, or otherwise removed on the parish night-soil cart; sometimes it was heaped up for sale later.

The lack of a convenient or reliable water supply was a crucial health risk. Many cottages relied on stagnant ponds or even ditch water. Halberton in the 1860s, as described to G.F. Millin by Canon Girdlestone, was all too typical:

> Numbers of the labourers' cottages unfit for the housing of pigs. Pools of stagnant water stand in different parts of the parish varied occasionally by stinking ditches. Heaps of manure thrown up under the windows of many of the dwelling houses. The whole village badly

drained; open sewers running through the place, frequently trickling down from the cottages into the brook, from which the villagers and the children often drank, and the cattle too. . . . The sanitary government was in the hands of the Board of Guardians, who were all farmers.

The best of the attempts at sanitary reform was that instituted by The Rev. Henry Moule, vicar of Fordington, which is now part of Dorchester. After outbreaks of cholera in 1849 and 1854, Moule turned his attention to the problem of sanitation and invented what he called the 'dry earth' system, which was extensively adopted in forward-thinking rural districts. The earth closet was said to fail because cottagers did not trouble to sift dry earth for use with them.

Little could be done to make most cottages healthy places to live. Lacemakers and strawplaiters ruined their eyesight doing intricate work in the dark, saving even the expense of the tallow candles and rush lights (and, later, oil lamps) which were the only means of illumination; damp brought pleurisy and rheumatism; cholera remained a constant threat; smallpox, scarlet fever, measles and whooping cough were common, consumption was rife. G.F. Millin describes a serious outbreak of virulent diphtheria at Quainton, Bucks, occasioned by the 'scandalously filthy' condition of the village, 'suggestive of the London slums'. The Aylesbury Board of Guardians, the responsible body, acted slowly, grudgingly and ineffectively, and it was left to Baron Rothschild, whose estate was nearby, to engage two nurses. In contrast to this official lassitude, the crisis brought out the best in the village notables:

> The village schoolmistress, Mrs Reeves, made heroic efforts to nurse the stricken children before the arrival of the nurses; and Mrs Cautley, the vicar's wife, had had an extremely hard and anxious time. The most unselfish and ungrudging assistance has also been given by the local squire, Captain Pigott, and Mrs Pigott. Infinite trouble and expense and worry, besides suffering and death, brought into many a poor home; and all might have been avoided if, when the people complained that they were being choked with foul smells, and their complaints were forwarded to their precious guardians, those guardians had paid as much attention as they would have done if they had had a hint that some poor hungry wretch had been snaring their rabbits.

The Boards of Guardians, who were responsible for the administration of the Union workhouses and of relief under the Poor Law, were much resented. Richard Heath recorded angry words from one Wealden woman:

> Only let me be a guardian for a week, and see what I'd do! Think of giving little children meat such as you would not give to hogs! Think of waking little children up at six in the morning, and not letting them have anything again until twelve! Would you like it? Of course they are hungry-like. Six hours be a long time for a child to wait. And then when they are sick, to have to apply to the Board, and perhaps wait a fortnight. It's a shame. Ah! that —— is a brute. I should like to scrunch him, I should. He *is* a brute.

The Boards of Guardians were responsible for employing a Poor Law medical officer for paupers. Often this was simply an extra duty for some hard-pressed general practitioner, but the best boards employed a man specifically for this post. Dr Thresh, for instance, was medical officer for the joint unions of Chelmsford and Maldon. He reported thus on the cottages at Ixworth, a village about four miles from Bury St Edmunds:

> These wretchedly small, overcrowded houses not only affect the morals but the health of the inhabitants. Rheumatism and chest affections are caused by sleeping and living in such damp, draughty dwellings. Infectious disease cannot be isolated, nor can any case of illness be properly treated in them. Apart from serious illness they are the cause of depression of vitality, generally affecting the bodily vigour as well as the spirits, and rendering the system unable to withstand the actual onslaught of disease.

There was a great need for cottage hospitals, but little will to provide them until the end of the century, when their numbers grew rapidly. Cottage nativities remained perilous affairs, with the attendance of a local woman as midwife for a modest fee.

The midwife might also double as a 'wise woman', dispensing herbal remedies and homely charms. William Clift, who was born in Bramley near Strathfieldsaye in 1828, of tenant farmer stock, recalled one such woman in his *Reminiscences*:

> Olive Sweetzer, 'the Whisperer', was most notable for her skill in nursing the women of the parish in childbirth. I believe she nursed my mother with most of her children. She used to 'whisper' away gathered fingers and other such diseases, and when anyone had the misfortune to run a thorn into their hand or finger they went to Olive Sweetzer to have it 'whispered'. Her custom was to wet her longest finger on her

tongue, rub the place over with it, and whisper, but what she whispered the patient must not know, or the charm would have no effect.

Although Clift does not mention it, Olive's ministrations were probably made with 'fasting spittle', before she had her breakfast.

In the main, cottagers treated their ailments, as Edwin Grey tells us, with 'salts and senna, brimstone and treacle' and with homely remedies made from herbs:

> Stewed groundsel was used for poultices, marsh-mallow leaves and flower made into ointment for boils, lily leaves for cuts, dock leaves for galled feet, green broom for kidney, and dandelion roots for liver troubles, coltsfoot leaves for bronchitis and asthma, rue pills for tonic, and so on, whilst the leaves of camomile, yarrow and agrimony were used for making what was termed 'Yarb tea', this tea being drunk for general health; lily leaves and also dock leaves were picked fresh and put on the sores straight away; sprigs of green broom, also the roots of dandelions and the coltsfoot leaves (these latter being dried a bit), were gently simmered in some water for a little time, and the liquor strained off and bottled, this liquor being used in the same manner as ordinary medecine. 'Yarb tea' was made in larger quantities, and sugared to taste. I have known some of the labourers take a quantity of this liquor in their tea cans for use in the fields instead of the ordinary tea.

Also, opium, for long freely available, was widely used in various preparations such as 'Godfrey's Cordial' and 'Daffy's Elixir', especially in fen districts where fever was endemic. In cases where nothing else helped, the local 'cunning man' might be applied to for a charm, which would be worn in a little bag around the neck. One such rhyme was universally held to be proof against toothache:

> Peter was sitting on a marble-stone,
>   And Jesus passed by;
> Peter said, 'My Lord, my God,
>   How my tooth doth ache!'
> Jesus said, 'Peter art whole!
> And whoever keeps these words for my sake
> Shall never have the tooth-ache!'

Despite such poor conditions and health care, the rural poor were stronger and longer-lived than their urban counterparts. As Richard Heath pointed out, 'under such a system none but the strong live', and those who survived childhood tended to have good constitutions. Working in the open air also contributed to good health. There were, then, in most villages, a good number of old people. With no old age pensions, the outlook for these people when their health failed was bleak. After a lifetime of hard work, the only option was the workhouse, which split husbands and wives, and was often at a distance of some miles from the home village. Richard Jefferies wrote that 'The workhouse and the poor-law system are inhuman, debasing and injurious to the whole country'; the union workhouses were known as 'Bastilles'.

After 1834, when out-door relief was discouraged, paupers were lodged in these strictly-run institutions, often presided over by ex-sergeant majors, where the sexually segregated inmates were set to work on such monotonous and menial tasks as breaking stones, crushing bones for bone meal and picking oakum. Most villagers made strenuous efforts to avoid the workhouse. The diarist George James Dew, Relieving Officer for the Bletchington district of the Bicester Poor Law Union, wrote in 1871 that 'every poor person in the land hates the name.'

But in old age, the workhouse loomed. It did provide for the physical needs of shelter, food and even health care in the infirmary, but it took away the self-respect of men and women whose whole lives had been, as George Sturt puts it, 'one continuous act of unconscious self-reliance'. Richard Jefferies deftly sketches the final act of the tragedy:

> When once an aged man gives up, it seems strange at first that he should be so utterly helpless. In the infirmary the real benefit of the workhouse reached him. The food, the little luxuries, the attention were far superior to anything he could possibly have had at home. But still it was not home. The windows did not permit him from his bed to see the leafless trees or the dark woods and distant hills. Left to himself, it is certain that of choice he would have crawled under a rick, or into a hedge, if he could not have reached his cottage.
>
> The end came very slowly; he ceased to exist by imperceptible degrees, like an oak-tree. He remained for several days in a semi-conscious state, neither moving nor speaking. It happened at last. In the grey of the winter dawn, as the stars paled and the whitened grass was stiff with hoar frost, and the rime coated every branch of the tall elms, as the milker came from the pen and the young ploughboy whistled down the road to his work, the spirit of the aged man departed.

Funeral expenses would probably be met by a burial club, the simplest form of the village friendly societies to which cottagers paid small premiums to insure against sickness, unemployment, and most important of all, a pauper's funeral.

While those above them enjoyed the substantial comforts of Victorian prosperity – the well-to-do farmers, writes Jefferies, 'have a joint twice or three times a week, well supported with every kind of vegetable' – the poor were schooled in hardship. One old woman told George Sturt, 'Well, 'tis only for life. If 'twas for longer than that I don't know if we should hardly be able to bear it.'

6

DRINK, BOYS, DRINK

❧ LEISURE AND ENTERTAINMENT ❧

We'll drink it out of the ocean, my boys,
Here's a health to the barley mow.
The ocean, the river, the well and the pipe and
    the hogshead, half-hogshead, the anker,
    half-anker, the gallon, the pottle, the
    quart and the pint and the half a pint,
    quarter-pint, nipperkin, pipperkin
    and the brown bowl,
Here's a health to the barley mow, my boys,
A health to the barley mow.
                    FOLK SONG ·

IN 1891, GEORGE FRANCIS Millin, a reporter on the liberal *Daily News*, discussed 'the stampede into the towns' with the Congregational minister of an Essex village. The minister told him:

> I don't think it's altogether wages. The country, you see, is very dull, and it is difficult to see how it can be made otherwise. The people have to be up at five in the morning and they require to be in bed by seven or eight o'clock.

The country is very dull. There one has, in its bluntest form, a basic truth of Victorian village life. For the cottagers, pleasures and recreations were simple and few. The nineteenth century saw a rapid erosion of traditional holidays and customs, with the replacement, for instance, of the old-fashioned Harvest Home with a cash payment. Augustus Jessopp noted in the 1880s that in Norfolk:

> There are scores – perhaps hundreds – of villages where the inhabitants have absolutely no amusements of any kind outside the public house,

where cricket, or bowls, or even skittles are as unknown as bear-baiting.

Even the public house, whether respectable inn or low pothouse, was a male preserve, and for village women there was no respite from family cares except for the exchange of the 'tittle-tattle and gossip' which Richard Jefferies characterised as 'their chief intellectual amusement'. While women's trivial chat is always called 'gossip', men's idle talk in the pub is dignified as 'conversation', and Jefferies, unlike many temperance busybodies, recognised that 'it is conversation that takes men to the public house.' In either case, the small minutiae of village life would be raked over and over with the same thoroughness as the leasing of a harvest field, till not a grain of interest or novelty was left.

One of the chief problems of rural leisure such as it was was that most villagers had nowhere to meet except the pub. In many English villages, the building of a village hall has only been achieved in recent years. With some honourable exceptions, squires and farmers alike disapproved of any social gatherings that were not under their aegis, where disaffection might thrive. While village inns, which the farmers themselves patronised, were seen as respectable places, the alehouses and beershops where the labourers drank were condemned as sinks of iniquity. Jefferies writes:

> It is a marked feature of labouring life that the respectable inn of the village at which the travelling farmer, or even persons higher in rank, occasionally call, which has a decent stable, and whose liquors are of a genuine character, is almost deserted by the men who seek the reeking tap of the ill-favoured public which forms the clubhouse of all the vice of the village. . . . Such a low house is always a nest of agitation: there the idle, drunken, and ill-conditioned have their rendezvous, there evil is hatched, and from there men take their first step on the road that leads to gaol. The place is often crowded at night – there is scarcely room to sit or stand, the atmosphere is thick with smoke, and a hoarse roar of jarring voices fills it, above which rises the stave of a song, shouted in one unvarying key from some corner.

After 'immorality', drunkenness was the prime target of Victorian reformers. In the last decades of the nineteenth century, temperance movements such as the Band of Hope were successful in persuading many children and adults to sign the pledge of teetotalism, and the dissenting chapels especially began to offer a rival social focus to the public house. Without doubt, those families where the husband was a teetotaller were both financially and emotionally better off, for drink then as now offered excitable temperaments an outlet for violence. The misery of cottage families in which the husband was a confirmed drunkard was very great. But of course many men who went to the pub in the evening merely nursed a pint for the duration; habitual overindulgence was beyond the means of most.

Spirits were rarely drunk. In their leisure hours, farmworkers stuck to the drink with which, as we have seen, the farmers made up part of their wages: beer or cider. Augustus Jessopp was told by an old Norfolk man that 'Gin came in with the railroad chaps.' Hubert Simmons in his realistic novel *Stubble Farm* shows women field-workers cajoling their master for 'a little drop of gin in the beer' as 'the wind do blow today', but it would have been the rare farmer who succumbed to such blandishments.

Village drunkenness has to be understood in the context of the general impoverishment of social life. As J. Millott Severn noted of the villages of Derbyshire, 'Drunkenness in these remote villages was a recreation for those to whom it had become habitual. Hard workers had little else to attract them.' His own father, 'a very hard-working man', was among those who went on periodic drinking sprees. Another was a 'hard-working builder', Mr Sheldon:

> Everybody in the village knew when Jimmy Sheldon had a drinking bout, for he proclaimed the fact wherever he went, and exultingly told the whole village again and again: 'Ah'm Jimmy Sheldon, you . . .! Ah'm Jimmy Sheldon!' which meant that he had a perfect right to do just what he liked without others' interference.

In common parlance this was – with a sort of mournful irony – 'to get as drunk as a Lord'.

Codnor, where Severn grew up, was chiefly a mining village. It boasted seven or eight pubs, of which the most popular was the New Inn, run by Mr and Mrs Thomas Clark. Severn gives a vivid picture of the social mix in this relatively respectable hostelry:

> Here in the evenings, sitting over their mugs and tankards of beer, smoking their short clays and talking, or playing table games, might be seen numbers of men, mostly colliers, stockingers and labouring men; whilst in the tap room was another better off class: pit gaffers, farmers, tradesmen and an occasional stranger or commercial traveller. The

landlady, smart, bright and ingratiating, with rustling silk gown, long gold chain and watch tucked in pocket at her waist, rings on her fingers, and cameo brooch fastening her dainty lace collar, usually served, and superintended this room, arrayed with shelves of shiny glasses, and portly kegs and bottles of spirits and cordials; and on a hanging board she chalked up the credit scores of customers. Here the monotony of dull days broke out into life with interchange of talk, snatches of folk songs, and some show of merriment, which would often continue until midnight and longer.

Flora Thompson in *Lark Rise* describes the singing which often enlivened the public house, ranging from contemporary music hall songs through the range of folksong to the positively archaic ballad of 'The Outlandish Knight':

> As this song was piped out in the aged voice, women at their cottage doors on summer evenings would say: 'They'll soon be out now. Poor old Dave's just singing his "Outlandish Knight".'

The importance of folk song to the rural community was very high. Folk songs supplied the village with a fund of narrative, humour, satire and social comment in a language everyone could understood and a mode in which everyone could participate. They could all join what Ginette Dunn's study of the pub singing tradition of Blaxhall and Snape in East Anglia calls *The Fellowship of Song*.

That fellowship was intensely local. Flora Thompson's acount includes a touchingly melancholy little verse which 'one comparatively recent settler, who had only lived at the hamlet about a quarter of a century, had composed . . . to sing when he felt homesick':

> Where be Dedington boo-oys, where be they now?
> They be at Dedington at the 'Plough';
> If they be-ent, they be at home,
> And this is the 'Wagon and Horses'.

The artistry of the singers of the Victorian village is still accessible to us through such early recordings as the seven discs of Joseph Taylor's singing issued by the Gramophone Company in 1908 at Percy Grainger's instigation. The expressive, unvarnished performances of such singers mediated and communicated deep feelings. At the inaugural meeting of the English Folk-Song Society in 1898, Kate Lee reported on the privilege of hearing James and Tom Copper singing in Rottingdean the previous year: 'I shall never forget the delight of hearing the two Mr Coppers, who gave me their songs. . . . Mr Thomas Copper's voice was as flexible as a bird's.'

That memory of delight helps to counter the truth of Percy Grainger's bitter testament, that so many singers 'died in poor-houses or in other downheartening surroundings . . . their high gifts . . . allowed to perish unheard, unrecorded and unhonoured.' Something of what the songs meant to the singers may be inferred from an aside muttered into Grainger's phonograph by one of those singers, frail Mr Deane of Brigg workhouse, as he strained his weak heart to do justice to the beauty of his melody: 'It's pleasin' muh.'

Men called on to sing who did not feel like doing so had a variety of short 'put-off' verses at their disposal, of a type also used by reluctant storytellers:

> I'll tell you a tail, the back of my nail,
> A pinch of snuff and a pint of ale.

The English storytelling tradition was already by the second half of the nineteenth century an impoverished rump of what must once have been a flourishing oral literature. The reasons for the decay of storytelling are complex, but the previously noted lack in English villages of any community gathering place (cottages being too cramped for socialising) was one strong factor.

Only a small number of *märchen* or fairy tales have been recorded in England, except from communities such as the gypsies where a more formal storytelling tradition survived. On the other hand, England is very rich in comic anecdotes, local legends, and stories of witches, ghosts, giants and fairies. These short, localised tales could be recounted off the cuff in many situations, and might be as brief and pungent as the remark of one old Wiltshire man to John U. Powell in 1895, 'I've heard 'em say that Adam were made and then put up again' a wold hurdle to dry.'

Stories were still told in the pub and in the fields, but the storytelling impulse survived most strongly in those who looked after children. Many of the English tales which were written down towards the end of the nineteenth century were recalled by well-off folklorists from the telling of rural nursemaids. These were sometimes variants of internationally known fairy tales, often of a grim or macabre cast, or else simple tales to point a moral. Richard Heath noted in passing, for instance, that New Forest children were reproved for greediness by means of the story of a forest girl 'who was in the habit of sharing her breakfast with a snake, and when he was inclined to lick up more than his portion, she tapped him on the head with her spoon, with this gentle reminder, "Eat your own side, Speckleback."' Even this tiny fragment of a tale is a version of a story told in many countries and known to folklorists as 'The Child and the Snake'.

Sidney Oldall Addy's *Household Tales with other Traditional Remains collected in the Counties of York, Lincoln, Derby and Nottingham* (1895) prints a representative collection of fifty-two unvarnished stories, but valuable as these are they are a ragbag of confused memories rather than the full record of a thriving tradition. Some of the distinctive stylistics of that vanishing tradition are preserved in other texts, for instance the oral version of 'Jack the Giant Killer' noted from eighty-year-old W. Colcombe of Weobley, Herefordshire, by Ella Mary Leather in 1909. His opening formula is one of the fullest recorded of such devices for entering and leaving the story world:

> Once upon a time – a very good time it was – when pigs were swine and dogs ate lime, and monkeys chewed tobacco, when houses were thatched with pancakes, streets paved with plum puddings, and roasted pigs ran up and down the streets with knives and forks on their backs crying 'come and eat me!' That was a good time for travellers.
>
> Then it was I went over hills, dales, and lofty mountains, far farther than I can tell you tonight, tomorrow night, or any other night in this new year. The cocks never crew, the winds never blew, and the devil has never sounded his bugle horn to this day yet.
>
> Then I came to a giant castle; a lady came out of the door with a nose as long as my arm. She said to me, she says, 'What do you want here? If you don't be off my door I'll take you up for a pinch of snuff.' But Jack said 'Will you?' and he drew his sword and cut off her head. He went into the castle and hunted all over the place. He found a bag of money, and two or three ladies hanging by the hair of their heads. He cut them down and divided the money between them, locked the doors, and started off.

One interesting feature of this narration is the way the verbal formulae enable the narrator to identify himself with the hero: '*I* went over the hills *&c.* . . . . Then *I* came to a giant castle; a lady came out of the door with a nose as long as *my* arm. She said to *me*, she says, "What do you want here? If you don't be off my door I'll take you up for a pinch of snuff." But *Jack* said "Will you?"' Mr Colcombe finished his tale with a simliar formulaic closure:

> Be bow bend it,
> My tale's ended.
> If you don't like it,
> You may mend it.

This storytelling style was as archaic by the close of the nineteenth century as such other elements of English folk culture as morris dancing and mumming. It was at this period, confusingly, that the educated classes started taking an interest in such things, and many customs on the edge of disappearance were revived by enthusiastic antiquaries. Hardy claimed, however, that you could always tell the difference between an authentic tradition and a revival:

> A traditional pastime is to be distinguished from a mere revival in no more striking feature than this, that while in the revival all is excitement and fervour, the survival is carried on with a stolidity and absence of stir which sets one wondering why a thing that is done so perfunctorily should be kept up at all.

Many traditional calendar customs, such as Plough Monday (the first monday after January 6th, on which bands of young men dragged a decorated plough around the district begging largesse, and in some areas performing traditional dances or a play), Pace-Egging (a similar Easter custom) and Souling (in which singers visited houses on All Soul's Eve or Day, asking for a 'soul cake' in traditional rhyme), were in many respects simply licensed begging. As such they were disapproved of and discouraged by vicars who were also unsympathetic to what they may have seen as pagan elements in the customs which had for centuries charted the rural year. There was, perhaps, something uncomfortable in a rhyme such as that chanted by the children of Eastleach in the Upper Thames on Valentine's day:

> Mornty, Mornty, Valentine!
> Blow the oats against the wind.
> We are ragged and you are fine,
> So please to give us a Valentine.

Christmas, of course, remained a key day in the year: the one day on which every family, however poor, tried to ensure that they had, as Edwin Grey put it, 'a good blow-out'. Ann Staight's diary entry for Christmas Day 1882 records Christmas in a comfortably-off household, complete with a visit from a band of mummers performing the traditional Christmas play:

> We had dinner rather late. Gave Mrs D's maid her dinner, Mrs D had hers from Rectory. After we had cleared, (Sis made fire in parlour) us girls washed and dressed and put on our best. Sis and I wore our jewellery presents (Annie gave us a pair of mittens each, and to the boys she gave two pretty boxes of matches). Annie helped us get tea, and all the 'boys' went up to Joe's to see after the cattle before tea; Louie, Alf, Sis, Tom and John went to church, Father went with Joe to his house. Annie and I washed up and cleared away, then came upstairs and she read 'The Letters' to me. . . . Later on the mummers came and we had them in the kitchen to act.

The other moment which remained of supreme importance in the countryside was the end of the harvest, although as the historian David Hoseason Morgan has clearly shown, from about 1880 decorous Church Harvest Festivals were widely substituted for the rowdier secular Harvest Homes of old. The harvest supper or horkey had pretty well died out by the turn of the century, as had the custom of 'crying largesse' in the harvest field, which gave the labourers cash to organise their own drunken 'frolic'.

The Rev. J.G. Fraser reported to the 1867 Royal Commission on the Employment of Children, Young Persons and Women in Agriculture that the songs sung at such gatherings were 'frequently obscene and disgusting'. The Earl of Albemarle attempted to substitute 'for the harvest frolic and its accompanying custom of largesse a monster tea-meeting, attended by from 2,000 to 3,000 persons, which it was hoped that the rustic mind, enlightened by some admirable addresses which were delivered on the occasion, might be brought to appreciate as "a more excellent way".' It was not a success: even at the monster tea-meeting, there was 'much drunkenness'.

It is too easy to laugh. The next page of Fraser's report notes a woman pleading with a fellow clergyman not to bestow largesse on her husband:

> My husband is generally good and kind, and seldom gives me an angry word; but after the feast provided by the 'largesse', he invariably comes home tipsy and gives me a good beating, which he never does at any other time. Ah sir, we women dislike the very name of 'largesse'.

Still, something vital to the self-respect of the rural community was lost in the abandonment of the old traditions of the harvest, even though these were, as Morgan makes clear, 'anachronistic in a wage economy'. Accounts of the old harvest suppers were always deeply nostalgic for a lost sense of sharing and celebration:

> There was master and missis a hippin an't up in front of us, and old Moll Fry a skippatin about with the cups. Presently all on us fell to. 'Lar, father, byent ye going to say grace,' missis says. Then master stood up, shet his eyes and put his hands together and said 'Oh Lard make us able, To eat all on the table.':
> 'Oh Dad, you wicked old fella!' cried missis, and all the young 'uns bawled out 'amen!' The parson purty nigh choked hisself with a lump of beef and had to wash it down with a cup of ale, and when they sang 'Drink, boys, drink' he said there was no need to tell 'em that, they could do that very well without being telled.

As they drunk, the toast would be, 'Here's success to the bright ploughshare, and may it never rust.'

Most villages had one other special day, that of the village feast, which celebrated the day of dedication of the village church. In Codnor in Derbyshire this was on the second Sunday in August, and was so important that it provided the focus for a whole week of merriment known as the Wakes. At Haddenham in Buckinghamshire, according to Walter Rose, the village feast on the nineteenth of September was celebrated with real zest:

> Long rows of stalls were put up, where every kind of delicacy to tempt the appetite was displayed, sausages, cakes and sweets, baked pears and nuts, and all for sale.

But this recalls a period before Rose's own lifetime. He was born in 1871, and by then many village feasts were being converted by vicars, as Richard Jefferies wrote in 1874, 'into a decorous "fete", with tea in a tent'. Jefferies gives a more typical account of village feast as 'two or three gipsies located on the greensward by the side of the road, and displaying ginger-beer, nuts and toys for sale; an Aunt Sally; and, if the village is a large one, the day may be be honoured by the presence of what is called a rifle-gallery; the "feast" really and truly does not exist.' In many villages, the feast owed its survival to the fact that village benefit societies fixed on that day as a suitable one on which to hold their club dinner.

Except in districts where the old 'mop' or 'stattice' hiring fairs still took place, giving occasion for much merriment and license, these tiny feast-day fairs were the highlight of many a rural year.

The amusements of the middle and upper classes were inevitably more sophisticated, and less tied to the pattern of the rural year, than those of the workforce. The Oxfordshire farmer John Simpson Calvertt's diary is fairly typical of his class. His main recreation was hunting, with the occasional day at the races or at a cricket match, the odd trip to London when he would go to the theatre, and games of whist and bezique with local friends. His scattered references to national and international affairs – such as the Zulu war – show that he was a close reader of the newspaper, but his interests were mostly very local, almost confined to his own farm. J.S. Fletcher writes of such men, in Yorkshire:

> Their lives were very simple; they were out all day on the land, keeping an eye on their men; at night they smoked their pipes, took their glass (a good many glasses), looked over the newspaper, possibly played a rubber of whist, and went to bed early. On market day they went to market; and now and then they went to fairs at York, or Leeds, or Selby, or Doncaster; once a year they went to the local show. . . . The exercise of social functions among this class was a matter of great solemnity and strict etiquette. There was very little visiting or calling done, and scant interchange of hospitality between families.

In politer households, recreations were equally decorous. Widely accepted middle-class amusements were reading aloud and singing at the piano; Ann Staight's relaxations were music, reading, sewing, crewel work, crochet, writing her diary. Croquet, and by the 1870s, lawn tennis (or 'sphairistike', as Kilvert calls it, judging it 'a capital game, but rather too hot for a summer's day') provided outdoor exercise, and picnic parties were also popular. Ann Staight went on one such expedition in 1875, on a visit to her friend Annie Biscoe in Enfield:

> Mr Biscoe had the grey horse and 4-wheel carriage and drove us up to Mr Gayfer's in the afternoon. We had tea in the hayfield, took up the things with horse and trap, the boy took up a faggot, we made a fire, boiled the kettle, had strawberries and cream etc. for tea. Afterwards we all went for a long walk over the farms to see the lambs.

Francis Kilvert gives a glowingly evocative picture of a 'jolly party' at Norton House, the Wiltshire seat of Sir John Awdry; 'almost everybody in the neighbourhood was there':

> I danced a Lancers with Harriet Awdry of Draycot Rectory, a quadrille with Sissy Awdry of Seagry Vicarage, a Lancers with Louise Awdry of Draycot Rectory, a Lancers with Mary Rooke of the Ivy, and Sir Roger with dear little Francie Rooke of the Ivy. How bright and pretty she looked, so merry, happy and full of fun. It was a grand Sir Roger. I never danced such a one. The room was quite full, two sets and such long lines, but the crush was all the more fun. 'Here,' said Francie Rooke to me quietly, with a wild, merrie sparkle in her eye, and her face brilliant with excitement, 'let us go into the other set.' There was more fun going on there, Eliza Styles had just fallen prostrate. There were screams of laughter and the dance was growing quite wild. There was a struggle for the corners and everyone wanted to be at the top. In a few minutes all order was lost, and everyone was dancing wildly and promiscuously with whoever came to hand. The dance grew wilder and wilder. 'The pipers loud and louder blew, the dancers quick and quicker flew.' Madder and madder screamed the flying fiddle bows. Sir Roger became a wild romp till the fiddles suddenly stopped dead and there was a scream of laughter. Oh, it was such fun and Francie Rooke was brilliant. When shall I have another such partner as Francie Rooke?

Other parties were more socially mixed. Mary Cholmondeley, for instance, recalled dances held for the village choir at Hodnet Rectory:

> We had a mixed choir, men, women and boys, and many a time we have danced with about sixty parishioners in the drawing-room of Hodnet Rectory, Father always leading off in the country dance with Mrs Cross, our principal soprano. My brothers and brother-in-law used to come in their pink hunt coats and dance all night with the village maidens.

More mundane village recreations ranged from the music of brass and string bands to the intricacies of bell-ringing; from penny readings, lectures and magic lantern shows to bowls, skittles, cricket and football; the old cruel sports such as cock-fighting had been made illegal in 1835, though no doubt there were isolated dog fights as there still are today.

Village cricket clubs thrived, and were one of the few areas of village life where members of different classes socialised together. One labourer in Sutton Courtenay, Berkshire in the 1880s, who had twenty-five children from two marriages, was able to field a family cricket team against the rest of the village. The 'Lady Farmer', Louisa Mary Cresswell, organised a team of village lads to amuse her son in the school holidays, thinking that 'besides the amusement, it is such a good way of teaching them fair-play and honour.'

As the century wore on, transport both by train and bicycle came within the reach of the workforce, and some villages began to organise annual day excursions. Hubert Simmons who was station master at Thame in Oxfordshire recalled how in the early days of the railway:

> The plough boys saved their money and had a ride from Princes Risborough to Thame on a Sunday, for the novelty of the thing. I have booked as many as fifty of these youngsters on one Sunday, who had no other object in travelling.
>
> My first pantomime did not delight me more than this ride delighted them, and they walked back eight or nine miles to whistle and plough, and talk about 'how trees and hedges rund along when "us" was in that thaire train', and how 'it frit I, when she went under the arch.'

Sunday was the day of rest. Most villagers would attend church or chapel at least once, and activities more boisterous than a train ride would have been frowned on in most communities. G.F. Millin gives a typically tranquil picture of the village Sunday in the High Wycombe area in 1891:

> Out again and along the gleaming white road, past the open cottage doors where babies in their best bibs and tuckers are seated on the mat, while father sits on guard just outside with his pipe. Doors are open back and front, and one can see through across the red-brick floor into the garden behind, still gay with dahlias and geraniums, Michaelmas daisies and marigolds, with here and there a well-laden apple tree. Rest – in perfect rest and quiet – that is the best way to express the manner in which all the villages seem to be spending the beautiful autumn Sunday.

Some villagers did manage to enjoy their Sunday more vigorously. For instance, Geoffrey Robinson's grandfather at Hedingham, while ensuring that his wife and many children went assiduously to church, did not himself attend except for 'hatches, matches and despatches': 'On Sundays generally he preferred to stay at home and make love to the maid.'

Drink, Boys, Drink

It cannot be stressed too much that the celebrations which punctuated the year went quite against the grain of daily life in the village, which was essentially quiet and often lonely. Augustus Jessopp writes:

> People who have lived all their lives in the streets have very little notion of the length of time that an agricultural labourer spends in solitude, or of the effect which this isolation produces upon him.

To villagers, everywhere beyond their daily round was foreign; a sense of the superiority of one's own community was sustained by the repetition of traditional jests and taunts celebrating the supposed failings of one's nearest neighbours. Visitors from outside this little world, especially those who were professional entertainers or who combined trade with showmanship, were eagerly greeted and long remembered. J.M. Severn recalled one particular cheap jack or travelling salesman:

> He had a van and stayed for months at a time, and every night drew large crowds. Hour after hour he would talk and joke, telling the funniest stories one after another, keeping his audience in a constant state of good humour and hilarity. He gave seemingly little time to the selling of his goods: just a rapid spurt now and then, when he would clear out a whole batch of his wares. Then a sudden halt, and he was back again to his storytelling. Many bought for the sheer pleasure of hearing him, and I think he enjoyed it himself. But he was not only humorous; he would give little lectures between the selling periods on John Bunyan and other serious and educative subjects; and he ingratiated himself with the chapel people, by giving them a lecture and attending their Sunday services. He was a short man, quick and alert in his movements, with dark flashing eyes, full of sparkling wit and merriment, and he could play the concertina and fiddle well, which he did sometimes as a diversion.

This talented and intelligent individual sounds the note of self-education and self-improvement which was such a strong force throughout the working classes in Victorian society. One of the most remarkable instances of this force in rural life was the example of James Wilkinson of Keld in Swaledale. Wilkinson, a local man who was also a Methodist preacher, started with twelve others a Mutual Improvement Society which in 1862 at the cost of £119 built and opened a Literary Institute in Keld, which is accurately described by Richard Heath as 'a miserable hamlet of about twenty cottages,

101

containing not more than seventy inhabitants, hidden in an out-the-way corner of the moors'. By 1872, Heath reported 'there is scarcely a village in Swaledale without its literary institute.'

Village reading rooms were one of the commonest projects of philanthropically minded aristocrats, but they were often regarded with resentment and suspicion by the villagers; in this case, however, local effort alone wrought a revolution in the intellectual life of a whole valley.

Where no Literary Institute existed, books were rare in the countryside, but newspapers, both local and increasingly national, circulated and were thoroughly digested. Richard Jefferies, pleading in his 1881 essay 'Country Literature' for a cheap reprint publisher who would distribute books to the countryside by post, remarks on the way in which country readers devoured 'everything and anything':

> The cottagers in faraway hamlets, miles from a railway station, read every scrap of printed paper that drifts across their way, like leaves in autumn. The torn newspapers in which the grocer at the market town wraps up their weekly purchases, stained with tallow or treacle, are not burned heedlessly. Some paragraph, some fragment of curious information, is gathered from the pieces. The ploughman at his luncheon reads the scrap of newspaper in which his bread-and-cheese was packed for him. Men read the bits of paper in which they carry their screws of tobacco. The stone-pickers in spring in the meadows, often women, look at the bits of paper scattered here and there before putting them in their baskets. A line here and a line yonder, one today, one tomorrow, in time make material equal to a book. All information in our day filters through the newspapers.

Even with the minimal leisure time available to a working man, some extraordinary villagers managed to pursue intellectual interests. George Baldry, author of *The Rabbit Skin Cap* poured a great deal of ingenuity into his attempt to invent a perpetual motion machine. The shopkeeper Benjamin Harrison was born in Ightham, Kent, in 1837 and lived there for eighty-three years, for fifty-four of which he kept the village general store. An ardent, self-taught archaeologist, Harrison kept a museum of his finds above his shop, corresponded with the great archaeologists of the day on equal terms, and made a considerable contribution to the subject; he was also a keen botanist and local historian. All this, Harrison achieved in his few hours leisure a week, with four bank holidays a year after 1872.

These were exceptional men, but by no means unusual. There was a real hunger for information, and also for imaginative literature. Geoffrey Robinson writes:

> Among the master craftsmen of the village, my grandfather and his cousin Charlie Rudkin were the intellectuals. Uncle Charlie was the more clever of the two . . . but grandfather himself was no yokel. He was sharply intelligent, scathing and intolerant. Any slow-witted though kindly man he dismissed as a 'ninny-nonny'. For his own education he read Pope, and considered 'An Essay on Man' to be the true philosophy. He was particularly fond of Shakespeare and liked Tennyson and Dickens. He read Charles Kingsley's *Hypatia* over and over again. For himself he took *Farm, Field and Fireside* and the *Cornhill Magazine*, and the children had *Cassell's Home Educator*, *Cassell's Magazine*, *Pearson's Magazine*, and the *Boy's Own Paper*. He encouraged them to think for themselves and opened their minds to the issues of the day. Conversation at meals was on serious and important questions.

Artistically, too, taste was developed by the London publications that filtered to the villages. The gawdy old coloured prints which had decorated many cottages began to be replaced by pictures from the *Illustrated London News* and the *Graphic*, featuring the work of the finest wood-engravers of the day. Hardy – whose own novels appeared serially in both these publications – recommended that such engravings be placed in schoolrooms.

Augustus Jessopp summarized the changes he saw about him in 1881:

> The truth is the peasantry have begun to have tastes as well as other people: they have shorter hours of work, *i.e.* more leisure; the women have almost passed out of the labour market altogether. I have found them reading novels; they like to see things looking pretty, they put up neat papers on their walls; *something* must cure the cracks and flaws that let the wind in; they buy pictures such as they are, they have an eye for art after a fashion. And all this is so much gain.

On the debit side, Jessopp thought, was the fact that the labourer had become 'more defiant in tone and bolder in his self-assertion'. Indeed, by 1881 that new self-assertion had already, in the labourer's agitation led by Joseph Arch, rocked Victorian rural society to its foundations.

7

OUR PROPER STATIONS

✌§ THE SOCIAL STRUCTURE §✌

O let us love our occupations
Bless the Squire and his relations,
Live upon our daily rations,
And always know our proper stations.
DICKENS *THE CHIMES*

VICTORIAN CHILDREN WERE required to recite a catechism which left them in no doubt that it was their duty 'To submit myself to my pastors and masters, and to order myself lowly and respectfully to all my betters.' No wonder that when the Rev. Francis Kilvert asked one child at Langley Burrell, Wiltshire, 'Who made the world?', he was answered, 'Mr Ashe' – the local squire.

The rich man in his castle, the poor man at his gate: this was the ordained social order of the Victorian village. To question it was to question God's will. But within that structure there was room for movement. It was easier, perhaps, to slip down than to rise up – for a smallholder to be reduced to labouring than for a labourer to acquire a smallholding – but examples of both could be shown. Many labouring families, like Hardy's Durbeyfields, cherished memories of better times.

Even the position of the landed gentry was not unassailable. Estates changed hands as they have always done, and many of the new owners – for instance Dearman Birchall, a Leeds merchant who in 1868 bought Bowden Hall at Upton-St-Leonard near Gloucester – were succesful businessmen rather than aristocrats: men for whom buying a sporting estate in the country was a way of buying social status.

There is no doubt that, with luck, thrift and hard work, the labourer could rise. G.F. Millin quotes a correspondent who describes himself as 'a man from the dunghill', who says, 'for years I worked at the roughest work done on the land, cleaning out pig-sties, turning manure, digging; and today, after twenty years of laborious work, I occupy the land I worked on and employ fifty hands.'

The rise of Isaac Mead, recounted in his *Life Story of an Essex Lad*, is instructive. He was born on 23 January 1859, into an industrious chapel family. He began as a labourer, but at the age of 17 applied for the post of assistant at a windmill, having heard that the previous man had been sacked for drunkenness:

> If you give me 1/- per day, just enough to buy my bread, and promise to learn me the trade, I will come to work for you for a term of years. You will not need me during the harvest months. If you will allow me four or five weeks during this time I can then earn a bit to buy me some clothes.

He was taken on, and worked in various mills till by 1882 he was looking for a mill of his own:

> In August, one Friday evening, I and my young lady, who was living in Chelmsford at the time, were out taking a stroll along the Baddow meads. I had got the Essex paper, and neither of us thought of any change in our positions. Suddenly I saw an advertisment that caused me to stop; I could scarcely believe my eyes. After reading it through to myself, I handed the paper to her, and I said, 'Mate, will you accept that as a home if I can hire it?' She, thinking I was joking, said, 'Don't talk so silly; however do you think you can hire that?'

He had for two years been investing in the Chelmsford Mutual Fund Association, which advanced him the money to hire Waples Mill, a run-down farm with both a windmill and a watermill. Although 'I certainly never anticipated such a struggle as I found I was in for', Isaac Mead managed to keep his head above water, and slowly advance, till when his autobiography was published in 1923 the Rev. Edward Gepp could write in his preface:

> Mr Mead is a successful man. Risen from the lowest grade of farm labourer, he has, by strenuous and intelligent exertion, become farmer, master miller, and owner of land.

Essentially, though, the social structure of the Victorian village was static, certainly compared to our fluid society. Everyone, from the squire (where there was one) to the labourer, knew their place. Farmers showed elaborate deference to squires, labourers tugged their forelocks to farmers. But within the workforce, there were many distinctions. Shepherds, for instance, were notoriously independent-minded and expected to be consulted by farmers about matters affecting them, such as how much spare hay should be kept. Craftsmen, tradesmen and men with responsibility over others such as bailiffs, gamekeepers and carters formed a class above the labourers, while among the workforce there were many who through some special skill lifted themselves into a better position. The basic farming skills such as ploughing, sowing and harvesting were not really regarded as skills at all, but those who were expert at such things as thatching, hedging and ditching, hurdle-making, or the treatment of sick livestock could expect improved pay and status.

In addition, the large Victorian village boasted a prosperous middle class, consisting of doctors, vets, solicitors, surveyors and auctioneers, wealthy farmers and, not least, retired gentlefolk, who leavened the social mix. Between aristocracy and gentry there was scarcely any distinction, the chief point being the owning of land rather the possession of a title, and many of the untitled county families priding themselves on their long pedigrees. Below them was a rank of independent country gentlemen, and below them the relatively prosperous middle class.

Between the upper working class, including craftsmen and small tenant farmers, and the labourers, there was as much sympathy and movement as between the wealthy farmers and the gentry. As Richard Jefferies writes in *Hodge and his Masters* – the fullest account of the rural middle classes – 'No man drinks the bitter cup of poverty to the dreg like the declining farmer.'

Jefferies saw that the old social organisation of the parish was disintegrating under the influence of fashion and town sophistication. Farmers' daughters – in a reiteration of an old complaint dating back at least to the prosperous years of the Napoleonic Wars – were beginning to 'play the fine lady',

> And the parish is splitting up into social cliques. These girls, the local leaders of fashion, hold their heads far above those farmers' sons who bear a hand in the field. No one is eligible who takes a share in manual work; not even to be invited to the house, or even to be acknowledged if met in the road. The Misses —, whose papa is well-to-do, and simply

rides round on horseback to speak to the men with his steam-plough, could not possibly demean themselves to acknowledge the existence of the young men who actually handle a fork in the haymaking time. Nothing less than a curate is worthy of their smile. A very great change has come over country society in this way.

One sign of this change was the increasing number of larger farmers who entrusted all dealings with their workforce to a bailiff, such as 'Old Monday', who was recalled by Flora Thompson:

> Sometimes afield, instead of the friendly shout, a low hissing whistle would pass between the ploughs. It was a warning note that meant 'Old Monday', the farm bailiff, had been sighted. He would come riding across the furrow on his little long-tailed grey pony, himself so tall and his steed so dumpy that his feet almost touched the ground, a rosy, shrivelled, nutcracker-faced old fellow, swishing his ash stick and shouting, 'Hi, men! Ho, men! What do you reckon you're doing!'

There were, of course, many differences in social relationships on the farm from area to area and even from farm to farm. In arable areas with large farms, the workforce, adrift in the cash economy, was more at the mercy of market forces and landlords' displeasure than in areas where smaller farms made it easier for the labourer to rent a smallholding of his own and enjoy a measure of financial independence.

The chief distinction to be made, though, is that between 'open' and 'close' parishes. In parishes with a resident squire, individual freedom might be curtailed to almost any degree. For instance, G.F. Millin writes of the 'close' villages of Kiddington and Glympton in Oxfordshire:

> I am assured that it is literally true that if in one of these places a young man wants to get married and settle down, it is of no use merely to woo and win the young woman. He must induce the squire to consent also. 'Where's So-and-So?' 'Oh, he's gone out of the neighbourhood. He wanted to get married, and the squire wouldn't put up a cottage and wouldn't hear of anybody taking in a lodger, so he had to go.'

Similarly, according to the King of the Norfolk Poachers,

> The Master would go to the man and say, 'Wich way you goen to vote John?' If the answer did not please him he would tell the man wich way he must vote, and John did it, or the Master made a spare man of him.

To many villagers it must have seemed their whole world was owned and ruled by the squire. For instance, in April 1843 Alexander Somerville visited the village of Strathfieldsaye in Hampshire, seven miles from Reading, the seat of the Duke of Wellington. He enquired of a labourer, 'The Duke must have a large estate here?' and was told:

> Yes, he have a terrible sight of land. I ha' heerd how many thousand acres he be owner of, but forget now; it be a many thousand. He be a buying land and never done. Oh! the Duke be owner of a terrible sight of land.

Even much less figures than Dukes expected absolute humility from their social inferiors. But as one Yorkshire labourer, or 'joskin', Arthur Tweedy, tells, humility did not always token respect:

> Whenever we met the squire or anyone else who thought himself a step above the farmers' joskins, we had to 'Sir' them and raise our caps and the ladies and girls had to curtsey. If you did not you were very smartly rebuked. I have seen women hide behind a hedge because they hated to humble down in this way. I remember asking my father why we should address them as 'Sir' and he replied, 'Sir, my boy, is only the nickname for a fool.'

Typically, the rector of the parish aligned himself with the interests and point of view of the squire and farmer. Richard Heath writes that, 'the rural clergy, as a class, have so closely identified themselves with the gentry as to give rise to the impression that they regard themselves as a sort of spiritual squirearchy.' This left them, according to Richard Jefferies in 1880, 'outside the real modern life of the village': 'The cottage folk just ignored the Church; nothing more and nothing less.'

As the 'Lady Farmer', Louisa Mary Cresswell, reports from Norfolk in the 1870s:

> The squires and farmers stand by the Church through evil report and good report . . . and many a dreary Sunday morning I have sat with frozen feet and hands through the drawled-out and gabbled prayers, the ill-sung hymns, and the tedious lifeless sermon, and how I have admired the old women in their long cloaks who really seemed to find some comfort in it all. But the labourers won't go to Church if they don't like the 'paarson', and vice versa.

G.F. Millin wrote in 1891 that 'half the evils of village life could be remedied if the parsons were worth their salt.' There were some remarkable and dedicated men in country livings, including such supporters of the labourers' cause as Canon Girdlestone, vicar of Hulberton, Devon, 'The Agricultural Labourers' Friend', The Rev. C.W. Stubbs, vicar of Cranborough and advocate of smallholdings, Charles Kingsley and his brother-in-law The Hon. and Rev. Sidney Godolphin Osborne. As representative of this class of clergyman, one might consider The Rev. William Bishop de Moleyns, vicar of Burrington in the Mendips, with a population of 467. He ran a parish school attended by 109 children, in which the farmers' children were taught side by side with the labourers'. Any promising child was found a situation as a gentleman's servant, a pupil teacher, a clerk in a merchant's office, a railway porter, or in domestic service. A 'Clothing Club' with contributions of 6, 4 or 2*d* according to circumstances bought shoes. The Lord of the Manor was persuaded to charge only a nominal rent for allotments.

Mary Cholmondeley's father, Rector of Hodnet in Shropshire, was typical of the best type of rural clergyman. He was entirely untroubled by the doctrinal controversies of the day, but devoted to the welfare of his parishioners, making no distinction between those who attended church and those who attended chapel. She writes:

> I cannot assert that he was a born priest, but he was certainly a born peace-maker. The parish with him at its head had a sort of homely but tough freemasonry. It held together, so to speak, of itself.

She gives a trivial, but impressive, instance of this 'peace-making' talent:

> I have known Father intervene with success in matters of extreme delicacy, as when one of Mrs Brown's caps spread on her side of the hedge to dry had 'got blowed' onto Mrs Jones's side, and had been appropriated by her; the situation, already grave, having been further complicated by Mrs Brown actually calling her neighbour 'Woman Jones' across the hedge. Possibly no self-respecting person, much less Mrs Jones, could restore a cap after that. Anyhow, Father probed the difficulty, obtained the cap, and took it back himself to Mrs Brown.

This sort of devoted work made a real difference to a village. But too often the sense of 'spiritual squirearchy' was too strong for any real contact between shepherd and flock. Even local charities when administered by most vicars were calculated to sap the self-respect of the recipients. G.F. Millin is writing here of a village in Suffolk, but it could be almost anywhere in England:

In the spring they all had to trudge up to the rector's wife with their charity blanket folded up in its bag to have it tied and sealed. They took their bags home till October, when they again went to the good lady to have their seals broken and the blankets released for winter use. Every cottager in the village had the loan of a blanket and seven hundred-weight of coal. There was a clothing club too, to which they all contributed, but everybody who went to town to buy clothing had to take the parcel from the shop straight away to the parson's wife, who would minutely inspect them to see if they were suitable for persons in their state of life.

The poor were divided into 'deserving' and 'underserving': the deserving were those who showed a proper gratitude for such charities, and who accepted their 'state of life' with due meekness. Some of the anger which such attitudes stirred up is expressed in the speech of a Wiltshire man from the 'Red Vans' of the English Land Restoration League:

> Our parson preach yesterday of we labourers being dissatsfied and discontented with our wages, murmuring of it, he said we labouring men ought to be satsfied with what we got. Be satisfied.

In 'open' parishes – which often, like Headington Quarry in Oxford, subject of an illuminating study by Raphael Samuel, had a reputation for roughness and crime – there was no one squire, but instead a number of small landowners and a substantial class of independent tradesmen and craftsmen, many of whom held and promoted radical views. Typical was the 'turbulent and irrepresible' radical shoemaker whom G.F. Millin met in Steventon, near Didcot: 'a Wesleyan "local preacher", a Sunday-school superintendent, a fighting politician, a regular "firebrand" among the labouring people about there.'

One district which – because of its impoverished soil – consisted largely of 'open' villages was the Sussex weald where the inhabitants, though poor, enjoyed, writes Richard Heath, 'a sort of crabbed independence'. The rector of one such parish told him, 'The people here wouldn't care twopence for a duke.'

The most contentious of all the areas of tension or conflict between master and man was poaching. The countryman regarded game as his birthright; the landowner, backed by the law, regarded it as his property. Hard labour in prison awaited anyone caught poaching or equipped for poaching, and the squires and parsons ('squarsons' in the contemptuous slang of the independent-minded) who sat on the Magistrates' Bench showed little mercy even to the very young and the starving.

The consequence was that poachers tended to be singled out as troublemakers. Once they had been before the bench, they found it more difficult to find work. As Joseph Arch recalled:

> It is a serious, a very serious, thing, because even if it is a first offence –
> it should not be counted an offence at all, I think – the man is looked on
> as a poaching vagabond by all the employing class round about. It is
> true that his neighbours do not desert him. I myself have taken such
> men along with me, as good men to work as ever took a tool in hand,
> but who after such a conviction could not get employment from the
> farmers. Well, I have gone with them from one end of the village to the
> other, to farmer after farmer, but nobody would give them a job. They
> have not had a farthing in their pockets, and what were they to do?
> 'Oh,' they would say, 'there's nothing for it but to go the whole hog.'

While casual poaching might amount to little more than knocking over a rabbit or hare with a well-thrown stone, or trapping them with a snare, or stealing eggs – or, in a gang, driving rabbits, partridges or pheasants into a long net – the poacher determined to 'go the whole hog' had very little reason to hold back when detected. The battles between keepers and poachers could be fierce, and men were frequently wounded and sometimes killed. In his *Autobiography of an English Gamekeeper*, the keeper John Wilkins recalls such an affray. Once they had him on the ground, the poachers kept him there 'with their knobbed sticks, thump, thump, like two blacksmiths at the anvil'. They pulled him from a ditch with the words 'kill the devil, let's drag him out and settle him', and his life was only saved by the intervention of another of the men, Jones, who was an out-of-work keeper himself.

The duties of the gamekeeper and the policeman overlapped. In densely keepered country such as Norfolk and Suffolk, where there were two or three times as many keepers as police, this is reflected in the proportion of poaching cases reaching the courts. David Jones in his essay on 'Rural Crime and Protest' in Mingay *The Victorian Countryside* notes that in Norfolk in the years between 1863-71, over 2,000 poachers were fined or imprisoned.

Most of these men poached out of poverty, but class resentment, and the excitement of pitting one's wits against the establishment, were also powerful motivating forces, for independent minded men such as the Oadby poacher, James Hawker:

> So much for the Sacred Game. There is no Man in England who Run more Risks, Been in more Dangerous Scrapes than me. Yet the only time I have Been in Prison was Not for Poaching but for getting a Poor Old widow woman a Bundle of Sticks as she had no coal. A Man who still Lives told the Keepers I had a Gun. It was a Long Piece of Ash, and they knew this Oadby man had told a Lie. But they sent me to Leicester Gaol for seven Days. They just thought it was time I was there. Ever Since then I have Poached with more Bitterness against the Class. If I am able, I Will Poach Till I Die.

The Poaching Prevention Act of 1862 was one of the most resented laws of its time, for it gave the police powers to stop and search anyone on suspicion, and lead to such ridiculous abuses of power as men being charged before the bench for theft of a few sticks from the highway. Joseph Arch remembered women from his village of Barford being stopped, searched, tried and convicted for theft of turnips, even though it was a traditional perk of the turnip fields that women cleaning turnips should have a few for their own use: 'It was a very great shame, and the village people were very bitter and sore about it.'

It can be argued, however, that tenant farmers, not labourers, were the worst sufferers under the game laws, their crops being devastated by preserved game, in the name of 'sport' for the landowner. Certainly Louisa Mary Cresswell, felt so. Her landlord, the Prince of Wales, was fanatical about shooting, and unwilling to pay proper compensation for damage and loss.

The rise of the rural police at this period, following the County and Borough Police Act 1856, was partly a consequence of the severe Game laws; ironically, just as it was said that poachers made the best gamekeepers, so too the police were drawn from the very class they persecuted. Many labourers were tempted by the better terms and prospects of police work, both in the rural and metropolitan forces. In Augustus Jessopp's Norfolk parish of Scarning, 'thirty-one sons of the soil have been enrolled as London policemen in thirty years'; they were, he wrote, 'the very pick of the parish'.

The village constable was in an uneasy position in the community, for while he was notionally the equal protector of all citizens' rights and property, he was in effect the representative of the landowners. George Sturt writes, of The Bourne in Surrey:

> There is probably no lonelier man in the parish than the constable. One hears him mentioned in those same accents of grudging caution which the villagers use in speaking of unfriendly property-owners, as though he belonged to that alien caste. The cottagers feel that they themselves are the people whom he is stationed in the valley to watch.

The conviction that there was 'one law for the rich, another for the poor' was deeply engrained.

The village policeman rarely had to cope with serious crime, though rape and murder were not unknown. Edwin Grey remembered that his village policeman, 'George Best the Bobby', dealt with 'nothing more startling than an occasional poaching affray, or fowl-stealing case, a public house fight, a neighbour's squabble, or maybe a few cases of petty theft, principally of fruit from some nearby orchard'. This list of trivial offences is typical of the late Victorian village, from which the violent impulses of the early century seem to have ebbed away.

The rick-burnings of the 1830s and 40s had subsided, and the machine-breaking 'Swing' riots with their heartbreaking aftermath of execution and transportation were little more than a folk-memory. Though ricks continued to be sporadically fired by arsonists with a grudge against particular farmers, and by tramps with a grudge against society, the resentful and delinquent found easier and crueller targets in the practice of animal-maiming. There was also ample opportunity for lesser vandalism. According to Jefferies:

> Intoxicated louts think it fine fun to unhinge gates, and let cattle and horses stray abroad, to tear down rails, and especially to push the coping-stones off the parapets of the bridges which span small streams. They consider it clever to heave these over with a splash into the water, or to throw down a dozen yards of 'dry wall'.

In most cases of disturbance, public opinion was inclined to agree with George Dew, a Relieving Officer of the Bicester Poor Law Union, that 'beer, that filthy beer, is the root of the evil'. While this was no doubt justified, it enabled the Victorians to avoid more uncomfortable truths about social injustice, and the simmering resentments of the workforce. These truths, which lay behind James Hawker's determination to 'Poach Till I Die', also animate Alexander

Somerville's conversation in the 1840s with a labourer he met at St Giles', the seat of the Earl of Shaftesbury:

> 'We be all like to have justice sometime; there ben't no noblemen in heaven, they say.' 'Is there not? and will there be any *poor* men there?' 'Not an the rich can help it; not an the rich can keep the poor out, I should think. But I be told no rich be to get there neither.' 'Who says so – the parson?' 'Oh, I ben't no friend of the parson's.' 'Why are you no friend of the parson?' 'The parson be no friend to me.' 'Why?' 'Because he ben't.'

Also lying behind this conversation is the influence of dissent, which grew rapidly in the labouring and upper working classes throughout the century. As Richard Jefferies saw, 'Dissent dissolved the connection between the lower ranks and the church, introducing a new centre especially their own.' He writes:

> At Bethel chapel between the services the cottagers, the farmers and the tradesmen break their bread together, and converse, and actually seem to recognise one another; they do not turn their backs the instant the organ ceases and return each to his house in proud isolation.

The chapel was distinctly felt by the squirearchy as a threat to the established order; G.F. Millin tells of a man in the Woodstock region who was given notice to quit his cottage, and turned out of employment, for having the audacity to hold a prayer meeting in his own room.

Louisa Mary Cresswell expressed a common view of Methodists when she wrote:

> They seem to think the groaning and howling on Sundays is an absolution for the sins of the week. . . . They make very good servants if you trust them with nothing, their wives are much cleaner and neater than Church people, and they keep their houses in the most exquisite order, and are respectful, friendly, and obliging.

The truth was that it was only in the chapels that the spiritual longings of the poor found an outlet. As J.S. Fletcher recalled from Yorkshire in the 1870s:

> The fact is that what was understood by the terms 'religion' and 'to be religious' was something which was supposed to be the strict prerogative of the Methodists. 'I'm a Churcher, always has been, and always shall be, 'cause I were brought up to it,' I once heard a woman say; 'but there's no doubt that the Chappilers is on much better terms with

Them Above nor what we are, 'cause they're more friendly with 'em, as it weer.'

Church of England parsons felt rivalled, and often personally offended, by the activities of the chapels. For many of them must have resented the difference between the frosty services in their own half-filled churches, and the enthusiastic meetings in the chapels. But the Rev. Augustus Jessop had the grace to admit:

> There is no denying that in hundreds of parishes in England the stuffy little chapel by the wayside has been the only place where for many a long day the very existence of religious emotion has been recognized; the only place in which the yearnings of the soul and its strong cryings and tears have been allowed to express themselves in the language of the moment unfettered by rigid forms; the only place where the agonized conscience has been encouraged and invited to rid itself of its sore burden by confession, and comforted by at least the semblance of sympathy; the only place where the peasantry have enjoyed the free expression of their opinions, and where, under an organization elaborated with extraordinary sagacity, they have kept up a school of music, literature, and politics, self-supporting and unaided by dole or subsidy – above all, a school of eloquence, in which the lowliest has become familiarized with the ordinary rules of debate, and has been trained to express himself with directness, vigour and fluency.

It was from that training that much of the rhetorical power of the labourers' movements was to stem.

8

WHITE SLAVES OF ENGLAND

✄§ VILLAGE RADICALISM §✄

Eight hours work
Eight hours play
Eight hours sleep
And eight bob a day!
UNION CHANT

THE MID-CENTURY agricultural labourer, dispirited after the tragic fiasco of the 'Swing' convulsions of the 1830s, was a docile figure. Workers did not unite for strength, but rather felt that, 'A man who cannot make his own bargain is not a man.' The 'King of the Norfolk Poachers' tells us that his father 'thought what the Parson and his Master said was always right. Perhaps they were, perhaps they were not, but not bein made beliven, as I got older I did not think as he thought.'

Those who 'did not think as he thought' gravitated to the new centre of village independence and self-respect, the Methodist chapel. Joseph Ashby of Tysoe, for instance, perceived early on that 'the labourers who could and dared make claims for themselves and their children were Primitive Methodists.' Methodism had sprung from the very class it served, and made Christianity a living force within the labouring community rather than a power over it. John Buck-master, in his *Memoirs of a Village Politician*, remembered from his childhood in the Chilterns how the methodists 'talked familiarly about Jesus Christ, as if He were a farm labourer keeping a family on nine shillings a week.'

Methodist meetings, whether in the little brick-built chapels which sprung up all over the country wherever local congregations could purchase a corner of land on which to erect one, or in prayer-meetings in cottage front-rooms, or in camp meetings in the field of a sympathetic farmer, were spirited, lively affairs which stressed the individual conscience. Arthur Randell describes a fenland meeting thus:

> Just as the Magdalen Baptists had an Anniversary Sunday every summer the Primitive Methodists always held a special Camp Meeting in a field where a farm wagon, surrounded by seats, had already been put up. There was a lot of hymn singing accompanied by a concertina and a fiddle and a number of preachers – known as Ranters – from all round the Methodist circuit would get up in turn onto the wagon and address the huge crowd. Before the evening service began the Methodists always paraded round the village singing at the tops of their voices as they walked, some of them backwards, a song which ran something like this:
>
> > I walked along the road one day,
> > I met a pilgrim on the way;
> > I said to him, 'Are you a planter?'
> > He said to me, 'No, I'm a ranter.'
> > Hallelujah! Hallelujah!

Men such as Joseph Arch learnt as Methodist lay preachers the art of rhetoric which fuelled their political success. Meetings of Arch's Agricultural Labourers' Union resounded to union songs set to hymn tunes, and the speeches were punctuated with outcries of 'Praise Him!', 'Lord have mercy!' and 'Amen!'. While Methodist hymns stressed eternal salvation rather than temporal justice, their rousing words and tunes encouraged a spirit of confidence, self-reliance and self-respect. As one chorus put it:

> We'll win the day – we'll win the day,
> Though death and hell obstruct the way:
> We only need to watch and pray
> And then we're sure to win the day.

The Primitive Methodists, though they saw society's manifest injustices, did not seek to inflame class antagonisms. Joseph Ashby remembered one preacher's words:

> Men are not equal. No! but they are brothers! Our neighbours on the farms and in the great houses be lucky and selfish and proud, and they expect you and me to put up with a lot of nonsense, but they be our brothers. Bitter in our hearts we are, but we can remember it; they and we be brothers.

But although Methodism was not itself a political movement, its lessons were crucial to the formation of countless mutual aid and educational groups in villages throughout England, as well as to the union movement. Primitive Methodism was in fact one expression of an urgent rural radicalism based in the larger open villages and led by craftsmen such as shoemakers and carpenters whose superior education and time for thought enabled them to establish rural talking shops – what M.K. Ashby calls 'street-and-smithy parliaments' – in which all the great issues of the day were discussed and analysed from the point of view of the working man. A Docking agricultural labourer named Sands wrote in 1874 to the *Eastern Weekly Press*:

> We are tired of landlord M.P.s and parson J.P.s They have been crushing us ever since we left Paradise. They got us down – feet, legs, hands, arms and shoulders. Our faces were crushed into the mud. We could not see. We have now just raised our heads, but they are resting still upon our hands. Our elbows are yet in the mud, but even in this position some of us are digging at law, others studying politics, others unions, and really it seems as though we intended mastering all the metaphysical enigmas of the day.

The spark which set off the fuse of union agitation in 1872 was simple desperation with living conditions. Wages had not risen from the nine or ten shillings a week of twenty years previously, and the labourers saw themselves starving in the midst of plenty. As one man from Wymondham in Norfolk put it:

> If they paid us well, they wouldn't ha' to come up to us during the day and say, 'There's very little work done.' What's the reason? Very often because a poor man's belly is empty. They say sometimes during harvest or haysel, 'So and So is knocked up and goen home. He's good for nothing.' What's the reason? 'Cos the master is putting money into his pocket that should ha' put food into our bellies.

But 'At last', writes the 'King of the Norfolk Poachers', 'wen things were a bad as they could be, Joseph Arch come along to be a Champion for Labour.'

Arch was born in Barford, Warwickshire, in 1826, of labouring parents, a man of great native intelligence and physical strength. Setting himself to master every aspect of farm work, he established himself as an independent labourer working at piece work 'at hedging and ditching and draining, at fence and hurdle making, at any and every job which would bring in good money', in the meantime 'pegging away at my books'. Combined with the fact that his parents owned their cottage, this enabled Arch to live comfortably, several rungs above the average poverty-stricken labourer. And because his home was safe, he could dare take on the squire and parson in a series of battles for individual freedom, earning himself the name of 'a contentious brawler, a dissenting wind-bag, and a Radical revolutionary': 'They gave me the bad name, but they couldn't hang me.'

Arch, then, was in a strong position to act when on 7 February 1872, in his forty-sixth year, two labourers, Henry Perks and John Harris, walked over from nearby Wellesbourne to ask him to hold a meeting at Wellesbourne that evening. They wanted to start a union, and were prepared, they told him 'both to fight and to suffer'.

When Arch arrived that evening at Wellesbourne, many hundreds of labourers had gathered, attracted solely by word of mouth, from villages within a ten-mile radius. Arch's memories of the occasion are couched in the Biblical terms which sprang naturally to so many of the labourers' leaders:

> By this time the night had fallen pitch dark; but the men got bean poles and hung lanterns on them, and we could see well enough. It was an extraordinary sight, and I shall never forget it, not to my dying day. I mounted an old pig-stool, and in the flickering light of the lanterns I saw the earnest upturned faces of these poor brothers of mine – faces gaunt with hunger and pinched with want – all looking towards me and ready to listen to the words, that would fall from my lips. These white slaves of England stood there with the darkness all about them, like the Children of Israel waiting for some one to lead them out of the land of Egypt.

Two or three hundred members were enrolled in the new union that very night.

Arch's National Agricultural Labourers' Union took off quickly. Soon he was speaking on village greens up and down the country and forming new branches wherever he went. The union was always strongest in Warwickshire and in Norfolk, where a long history of radicalism quickly seized on this new opportunity, and where the union had one of its ablest organizers, George Rix.

Farmers reacted quickly and decisively to the threat of organised labour. Men known to have joined the union faced instant dismissal. But instead of cowing them into surrender, this stiffened the men's resolve, and on 11 March the Wellesbourne labourers struck. The strike lasted a bitter month, and at the end of it the farmers were offering wages of fourteen, fifteen or sixteen shillings a week to those labourers who had not taken advantage of the much better paid work they had been offered in factories and docks in other parts of England, and even on the railway in New Zealand at seven shillings a day.

A series of local strikes and lockouts in the coming months was widely reported in a press almost wholly hostile to the union's 'agitation'. When the labourers at Wootten in Oxfordshire formed a union, they raised wages from ten shillings a week to eleven and then twelve, but when they asked for sixteen they were locked out, a hundred and twenty men were thrown out of work, and soldiers of the 46th Foot were sent from Aldershot to get in the harvest. When the vicar at Coombe in Hampshire had the courage to preach in favour of Arch, the churchwardens, who were farmers, locked him out of the church, preventing him from preaching for several weeks.

Arch himself felt 'as if there was a living fire in me'. One of Francis Kilvert's old parishioners at Langley Burrell told him a revolution was coming: 'I know it's coming, as sure as this prong is in my hand.' Not everyone could adjust to this new force in the village. One old man in South Warwickshire – Arch's stronghold – told Richard Heath:

> I don't think much o' this 'ere Union, and I'll tell yer why, sir. Here have I served one man or his father this forty year, and never had a misword. All the work I have done he's paid me for. How do you think, sir, such a maayster 'ud like it if I was to fly in his face and ask for more wages? We must all do our duty, sir. The maaysters must do their duty to the men, and the men must do their duty to their maaysters. England expects every man to do his duty, sir, as Lord Nelson said.

Arch was an indefatigable speaker, and it is possible from various accounts to reconstruct a typical meeting. Arch would be introduced to the audience by some local leader, often an elderly man with less to suffer from being singled out as a troublemaker. One said:

> Summat should be doin' for the lab'rin' class. I've no hope for myself, but afore I dies I'd uncommon like to see the young uns doin' better'n I've done.
>
> I've herd o' the Wellesbourne men, and Muster Arch, and seein' as the master and the squoire canna greatly harm me, sin I'm nigh done, I've made bold to ax Muster Arch to come and tell 'em down here what

they must do to get a trifle more wage and a bit better food, and Muster Arch, like a good un as he is, has come and will speak himself.

Arch typically mounted the platform to the strains of 'See the Conquering Hero' from the village band. His style was blunt and direct. He would tell his audience, 'I am a working man – one of yourselves', and exhort them 'Now, working men, get the wool off your eyes.' He wanted them, he would say, 'to see that you are men and not machines.'

Thomas Hardy heard Arch speak at the Dorchester hiring fair in 1873:

> The picture he drew of a comfortable cottage life as it should be, was so cosy, so well within the grasp of his listeners' imagination, that an old labourer in the crowd held up a coin between his finger and thumb exclaiming, 'Here's zixpence towards that, please God!' 'Towards what?' said a bystander. 'Faith, I don't know that I can spak the name o't, but I know 'tis a good thing,' he replied.

It was on just such 'zixpences' that Arch's union thrived, and on which it foundered.

The immediate success of the union, raising wages by about 40%, and as high as fifteen or sixteen shillings in some areas, encouraged unrealistic expectations from the labourers. Arch remembered, 'A number of the hasty and too eager ones thought the Union was going to do everything for them all at a stroke; they were just like a crowd of greedy, impatient children.' As one disenchanted labourer put it:

> They will have no more of my twopences. . . . I thought by his account we were going to have a lot of land, but it's him that's the gentleman, and we have to work hard for it.

Employers – who, like Louisa Cresswell, regarded Arch's movement as 'a violent communistic attack upon property' – encouraged the notion that union subscriptions went straight into Arch's pocket; wives would ask their husbands 'why we wanted to keep ol' Joey Arch a gennelman'. So amid a flurry of wild – and as the surviving accounts show, untrue – accusations about misuse of funds, the union collapsed, weakened as it was by more direct challenges in the form of farmers' lock-outs and evictions from tied cottages, as well as by the reduced demand for labour as the agricultural depression hit. Arch's union was only really effective in its first decade, and when the end came in 1896 it had dwindled almost to nothing.

It was all a far cry from the first heady days when full-throated gatherings of labourers roared out such union anthems as 'When Arch beneath the Wellesbourne Tree':

> When Arch beneath the Wellesbourne tree
> His glorious work began
> A thrill of hope and energy
> Through all the country ran.
> But farmer, parson, lord and squire
> Looked on with evil eyes;
> Some looked with scorn, and some with ire,
> And some with dumb surprise.

In conversation with Tom Higdon in 1909, Arch commented bitterly, 'the union went down – and the wages went down with it. The union was *wrecked*. They broke up their union and left me without a penny.'

Higdon was an official of the successor to Arch's National union, founded in Norfolk in 1906 by George Edwards, who had been a branch official in Arch's union. Radicalism had been firmly established in Norfolk before Arch, and indeed in 1879 the Norfolk labourers had split from the National union to form the Norfolk Federal Union under George Rix. Edwards's union, building on the foundations of Arch's, developed into today's National Union of Agricultural Workers.

One of the influential men who did support Arch's union was Canon Edward Girdlestone, rector of Halberton, Devon. Girdlestone had taken the opportunity when a cattle plague was at its height in 1866 to preach a sermon at Halberton Church in which he asked the congregation whether they did not think the plague a sign of God's displeasure at the farmers' treatment of the labourers. He caused an uproar, with anonymous letters attacking him in the local press, and a resolution passed at the annual tithe dinner, when the time came to propose the vicar's health, that the glasses instead of being filled should be reversed empty. Girdlestone wrote to *The Times* outlining the condition of the labourers, and with the donations he received started a migration scheme sending men to other counties. Men who were working on the land for starvation wages of eight shillings a week were sent for instance to join the Manchester and West Riding police forces, receiving between thirteen and twenty-two shillings a week plus good cottages and gardens rent free.

This idea of Girdlestone's, 'carried out in single-handed conflict with nearly the whole district of squires and farmers', developed in Arch's hands into an organised emigration scheme which sent many thousands of families out to new jobs in Canada, Australia, and New Zealand. This drain of skilled workers to the dominions – and yet more to the United States – was to have grievous repercussions for English agriculture in years to come. In a speech in 1879, Arch said:

> You have a right to ask who were the men who went? They were those with the most courage, and those whom the farmers could least do without; those who could and would turn their hand to anything. The very men that the farmers said seven years ago they would starve into submission, are those who are now helping foreign growers compete with farmers at home.

One key area of contention was over the question of allotments. In *Joseph Ashby of Tysoe*, M.K. Ashby shows very clearly how basic to the survival of the village as a working community was the fight for village allotments, which gathered momentum through the 1880s with the formation of many Allotments Associations. Farmers were often reluctant for their men to have allotments, on the grounds that work which should be going into their crops would be diverted into the labourer's own. Where allotments were available, they were always taken up, even though they were frequently inconveniently situated.

F.G. Heath noted in the 1870s that while some farmers who rented allotments were fair, most took advantage of the labourers' eagerness to rent on any terms. He instanced Henry R—, a labourer earning nine shillings a week in 1872 in the village of North Curry in Somerset. He had a wife and six children, and his cottage cost him £4.6s a year. He rented a quarter of an acre of potato ground at a rent of £2.5s from a farmer who was himself paying £2.10s an acre, and therefore charging the labourer four times his own rent.

In contrast to this, forward-thinking parsons were often prominent in fostering allotment schemes. For instance, in 1873 The Rev. Charles William Stubbs, vicar of Stokenham, Bucks, believing that the future of the village depended on an increase in small-holdings, divided twenty-two acres of his glebe land into half-acre allotments among his labouring parishioners at an annual rental of £3.6s an acre, retaining one acre in his own hands to work in the same way as the rest.

The Tysoe allotments, 'the Promised Land', were finally achieved in 1893. On a larger scale, the Smallholdings Acts of 1892 and 1908 attempted, with limited success, to keep labourers on the land by turning them into small-scale farmers in imitation of the continental peasantry. Allotments were now officially encouraged. But it was probably too little too late.

The Tysoe struggle, in which the Vicar and the farmer Trustees of the charitably-endowed 'Town Lands' stood resolutely in the face of progress, also exemplifies the inadequate nature of the existing village political institutions. The old power of the Vestry had declined and been subverted by class interest, and there was no new village organisation to offer the community a voice in its own government. Parish Councils were not formed until 1895 when the Local Government Bill was passed in amended form, having been emasculated by the Lords who feared, as M.K. Ashby puts it, that 'the Bill would promote a village leadership which was not that of the land owner or of the incumbent whom he could influence.'

Richard Jefferies in his essay 'After the County Franchise' had argued that a 'sense of independence can only arise when the village governs itself by its own council, irrespective of parson, squire, tenant or guardian.' The extension of the franchise to the rural labourer in 1884 was, as Jefferies fully realised, also a crucial ingredient of this independence. On 8 December 1885, Joseph Arch was returned as Liberal Member of Parliament for North-West Norfolk, polling 4461 votes to Lord Henry Bentinck's 3821.

With national victories such as this, and local ones such as the Tysoe 'Promised Land', the balance of power in the village began to tilt. As Arch's members sang:

> They thought they'd kept us down so low
> Our manhood was starved out;
> So ignorant, we should not know
> The task we were about.
> But now no longer they despise
> The men who strive with wrong;
> Whom they thought fools, they find are wise,
> Whom they thought weak, are strong.

As James Hawker put it:

It is often said the agricultural labourer seemed a Deal Happier 60 years ago that what they seem to Day. Well, we know there are many men Better off in Prison than what they are out. But they would Rather be out.

9

CHANGE IN THE VILLAGE

✥ A WORLD IN FLUX ✥

Here's a health to the world, as round as a wheel,
Death is a thing we all shall feel;
If life were a thing that money could buy
The rich would live and the poor would die.
TRADITIONAL

IN 1902, THOMAS HARDY wrote to Rider Haggard about the changes he had seen in Dorset villages over half a century. Most notable was the improvement in living standards for the workfolk. He wrote:

Their present life is almost without exception one of comfort, if the most ordinary thrift be observed. I could take you to the cottage of a shepherd, not many miles from here, that has brass rods and carpeting to the staircase, and from the open door of which you hear a piano strumming within. Of course, bicycles stand by the doorway, while at night a large paraffin lamp throws out a perfect blaze of light upon the passer-by. The son of another labourer I know takes dancing lessons at a quadrille class in the neighbouring town.

But such material benefits, representing in brass rods and dancing lessons the labourers' first tentative encroachments on the comforts and refinements of the middle class, were accompanied, wrote Hardy, by 'other changes which are not so attractive'. In particular:

The labourers have become more and more migratory, the younger families in especial, who enjoy nothing so much as fresh scenery and new acquaintance. The consequences are curious and unexpected. For one thing, village tradition – a vast amount of unwritten folk-lore, local chronicle, local topography and nomenclature – is absolutely sinking, has nearly sunk, into eternal oblivion.

The old stability of village life, which was to receive its quietus on the bloody fields of the Great War, was already fatally undermined.

Hardy attributed the greater mobility of the rural population, and especially the migration to the towns, primarily to 'insecurity of tenure'. But while, with many cottagers and tenant farmers liable to summary dismissal, this was clearly a major factor, there were other forces at work. One of these was that the building of new roads, and the coming of the railways, simply made travel easier for all. The inertia of the old village life was partly caused by the sheer difficulty of transport. The village post office was another key factor in opening the villages up to outside influences. In many ways, the post office can be seen as taking over from the church or the manor house as the focus of village life.

Hardy's sense of loss was real. No man in England would have been less prone to nostalgia for the passing of an imagined rural idyll. His sorrow was rooted in his understanding that what was passing had never been valued at its true worth. He strikes a note echoed by George Sturt in a journal entry for 28 May 1906:

> Though there was much that was good, it was bought too dear. I think especially of the peasantry. The women grew prematurely old: the children early lost their charm: the loveliness of the girls was gone almost before they had grown up. One may judge it, by those amongst whom the old mode of living still survives. The waste of beauty is heart-rending.

Indeed, the loosening of community ties, and the new sense of impermanence and change which informed village life, were not wholly to be regretted. Broader mental horizons enabled villagers to move beyond – or simply move away from – the 'stagnation and narrowness of mind' which Jefferies saw as souring village life. He wrote:

> Backbiting is the curse of village life, and seems to keep people by its effects on the mind far more effectually in the grip of poverty than the lowness of ways. They become so saturated in littleness that they cannot attempt anything, and have no enterprise.

On the other hand, Jefferies too saw draw-backs in the break-up of the old village life and the dispersal of the villagers. Writing for a middle-class readership in 1880 he was dismissive of the 'airs' of cottage girls, who began to dress fashionably and seek to better themselves in marriage, and disturbed by the 'coarse cynicism' picked up by young labourers who roamed the countryside at casual jobs. He writes:

> Had any one gone into a cottage some few years back and inquired about the family, most probably the head of the house would have pointed out all his sons and daughters engaged in or near the parish. Most likely his own father was at work almost within hail. Uncles, cousins, various relations, were all near by. He could tell where everybody was. Today if a similar enquiry were made, the answer would often be very different. The old people might be about still, but the young would be found scattered over the earth. One, perhaps, went to the United States or Canada in the height of the labourers' agitation some years ago, when agents were busy enlisting recruits for the Far West. Since then another has departed for Australia, taking with him his wife. Others have migrated northwards or to some other point of the compass – they are still in the old country, but the exact whereabouts is not known. The girls are in service a hundred miles away – some married in the manufacturing districts. To the middle-aged, steady, stay-at-home labourer, the place does not seem a bit like it used to. Even the young boys are restless, and talking of going somewhere. This may not be the case with every single individual cottage family, but it is so with a great number. The solid phalanx of agricultural labour is slowly disintegrating.

One further cause of this disintegration was the fact that with increasing mechanisation from the 1870s on, fewer labourers were needed on arable farms (though this was offset to some extent by new demands for labour caused by more intensive farming and greater use of horses). George Dew's diary note for 28 July 1870 tells the story succinctly enough:

> W.P. King who holds the better part of the Rectory Farm beside other land has a new reaping machine which cost near upon £30. I saw it today & it does its work well. He says he can save 4/- an acre in the expense of cutting his corn, & it is calculated to do the work of sixteen men with only one man and two horses, but it might perhaps be nearer the truth if it were set at 12 men, & this I think is not overstating the mark. This of course is well for him but the labourers are cut out of work, & it transfers labour from agricultural labourers to engineering mechanics.

133

By 1880, Richard Jefferies was writing of village 'factories', run by 'machinists': men who owned, rented out and repaired steam ploughing machines. The stage was set for the conversion of the village smithy into the village garage.

Of course the industrialized village was no new thing. J. Millott Severn's Codnor was typical of many such villages in which agriculture was very much a peripheral activity. As he recalled:

> The chief industries of this village, consisting of only a few hundred inhabitants when I was a boy, were ironstone and coal mining, stocking, weaving, and employment in the Butterley Company's iron works at Codnor Park; there were also a few surrounding farms.

The nature of such villages remained, despite the decay of some old rural trades and crafts such as ironmaking, textiles and framework knitting, more static than that of previously rural and remote communities whose inhabitants suddenly had a choice of occupations where previously there was none, with the rapid spread of rural quarries, brickworks, cement works, railway years, furniture factories, feed mills and so on. A good example is that of the villages around Swindon, once the Great Western Railway Works opened there. Many of the villagers were tempted away from the land by the higher wages available for factory work. Alfred Williams, who lived in the village of South Marston, worked as a hammerman in the steam hammer shop. As he recalled, workers from such outlying villages needed an early start to get to work on time:

> Soon after four o'clock, in the quiet hamlets amidst the woods and lanes, the workmen will leave their beds and get ready for the long tramp to the shed, or to the nearest station touched by the trains proceeding to the railway town.

As time went on, the younger workers acquired bicycles for the journey.

There was in such factories a certain amount of rivalry between town and village dwellers, particularly at times such as harvest when the villagers could supplement their income with work in the fields. As Williams explains:

> It was the custom . . . during haymaking and harvest-time for farmers to come in with conveyances from the outlying villages and meet the men and drive them home. They went straight from the factory to the farmyard or hayfield, and, after a hearty tea in the open air, or a square

meal of bread, cheese and ale, turned in and helped the farmer, both enjoying the change of work and earning a couple of shillings a night as additional wages. This practice was very popular with the factory men, who never ceased to talk about it to their town mates in the shed and rouse them to envy with their frequent narration.

On the other hand, for countrymen such as Williams the noise and monotony of the factory work contrasted badly with agricultural labour; in his second letter to *The Times* in 1872, Richard Jefferies claims that village labourers who obtained positions at the G.W.R. Works 'usually, after a short period return to farmwork'.

The railways also offered alternative employment as navvies in the construction of new lines. Hubert Simmons's novel *Stubble Farm* reconstructs the gleeful conversation of a group of village wives anticipating the coming railway:

'Well, so the railway's a-comin; and thank God for't.'

'Yes. and Tom's got 'is name down at Tug and Tickle's to go and teach the boys how to run the tip-trucks what's going to make the 'bankments, and he's to have five shillings a day to start with.'

'Well, I only wish my old man was a bit younger, he shouldn't cut no more chaff in that barn for ten shillings a week; but I'm afeard that railway job will only last a year or so, and if he leaves now our master won't take him back again, and then where will he get another reg'lar place?'

'My husband's a-going.'

'And so's mine.'

'They be all a-going to give notice next Saturday, and shouldn't I like to see old Tom Strong when they tells him; won't it be a spree? Just as if they're a-going to wop that straw about, for ten shillings a week, on a crust of bread and cheese and a honion, when they can 'ave four-and-sixpence a day, and make enough overtime to buy beer, a-making this railway.'

Better wages were not the only attraction of work on the railways. Navvying was also a freer, more independent existence. Mark Thurston of Essex recounted a story to C. Henry Warren about his father, who when out ploughing was approached by the Squire and accused of whistling to warn his mates of their employer's approach; in fact it had been peewits calling. The Squire forced him to admit to the crime, on pain of the sack. Mark's father, 'one of the strict sort', returned home 'savage', insisting that 'I'll show 'im':

And sure enough, that very summer father 'eard they were buildin' a railway down Dunmow way; so one mornin', instead of gooin' to wukk as usual, he cleared off up to the Hall. Right up to the front door he went. 'Is it anything perticler?' asked the servant who answered his ring. 'Yes,' said father, 'very perticler, tell 'im.' Presently Squire came out to see what all the fuss was about. 'Do you remember that time I was ploughin', back in March,' said father; 'and you asked me why I whistled to warn my mates that you was a-comin'? And do you remember I said I hadn't done no such thing? Nor I hadn't: it was them peewits. But you made me tell a lie. So I've come up here this mornin' to tell you what *you* did was worse'n any lie. You bullied me; but you shan't bully me no more. I'm gooin' to wukk on the railway. Good mornin', Squire!'

This lovingly rounded anecdote, with its splendidly satisfying denouement, gives an indication of the extent to which such slights and humiliations were resented and brooded over.

The old-fashioned arrogance of the squirearchy was, anyway, on the way out. As the villages opened up to the outside world, so the dominance of the local landowner became less absolute. The station-master, for instance, was a new element in village society who owed no special allegiance to the squire. The first railway clerks and stationmasters were drawn from the middle classes, and though they were rapidly replaced by upwardly-mobile workers, nevertheless they did not fit in to the established hierarchy, and needed propitiation even from the great. As Hubert Simmons put it, '"My Lord" knows he has no right to bully at the station, so he brings up a brace of pheasants, and thus adds Mr Station Master to the train of his servants.'

The middle class element in villages increased strongly in the later years of the century with the building of speculative villas, and the custom of hiring summer homes in villages also steadily increased. Richard Jefferies writes:

This practice of hiring a village home for the summer has been common of recent years among the leading tradesmen of country towns. Such visitors are welcome to the cottage folk. They require the service of a labourer now and then; they want fresh eggs, and vegetables from the allotment gardens. The women have the family washing to do, and a girl is often needed to assist indoors, or a boy to clean the knives and shoes.

Such fringe improvements to village labour prospects could not, however, stem the 'stampede into the towns'. The landlady of an Essex inn told George Francis Millin in 1891, 'As soon as the young 'uns be able to do for theirselves, they be off to better theirselves as they think. They go into the towns and get into the police or the army, or on the line.' Talking to three sisters in a 'low-raftered, pokey little' cottage, Millin ascertained that all three had been in service and were only temporarily back at home. 'You wouldn't catch us settling down here', they told him.

Another woman told him why her son had left:

Well, sir, he couldn't save nothing out of his pay. All through the winter he got ten shillings a week, and when he'd paid me for his board and lodging and had dressed himself – he is a young fellow of two-and-twenty, and dresses pretty well – there was nothing left. 'Mother,' he says, 'I shall never be better off at this game. I'm a goin to try my luck in London.' . . . He went over somewhere down Penge way and got on at once with a contractor or some't to drive a cart at a pound a week, but he soon giv that up and got on to the railway. I ain't quite sure what he gets there, but I know it's over a guinea.

Social distinctions had begun to blur. Improved transport and communications had opened the villages out to wider influences. Mechanisation of farm labour, and wages held low by agricultural depression, reduced the need for farmworkers and made new alternative employment more attractive, especially for the more bright and ambitious youngsters. By the end of Victoria's reign, the old patterns of village life were all breaking under the strain, and would soon be all but swept away. The war memorials which rose on village greens throughout the land after the cataclysm of the Great War, with their poignant lists of the old village names – four from this family, three from that, two from another – were memorials, too, to a way of life which was gone for ever.

It was more of a memorial than the village poor were used to. They lived and died for the most part unknown and unregarded; the few whose haphazardly recorded words I have quoted in this account of their vanished world must stand for countless others who will keep their accustomed silence for eternity.

It seems fitting then to close, without comment, on W.H. Hudson's conversation in a Wiltshire churchyard:

I went over to the stone she had pointed to and read the inscription to John Toomer and his wife Rebecca. She died first, in March, 1877, aged 72; he in July the same year, aged 75.

'You knew them, I suppose?'

'Yes, they belonged here, both of them.'

'Tell me about them.'

'There's nothing to tell: he was only a labourer and worked on the same farm all his life.'

'Who put a stone over them – their children?'

'No, they're all poor and live away. I think it was a lady who lived here; she'd been good to them, and she came and stood here when they put old John in the ground.'

'But I want to hear more.'

'There's no more, I've said; he was a labourer, and after she died he died.'

'Yes? go on.'

'How can I go on? There's no more. I knew them so well; they lived in the little, thatched cottage over there, where the Millards live now.'

'Did they fall ill at the same time?'

'Oh, no, he was as well as could be, still at work, till she died, then he went on in a strange way. He would come in of an evening and call his wife. "Mother! Mother, where are you?" you'd hear him call, "Mother, be you upstairs? Mother, ain't you coming down for a bit of bread and cheese before you go to bed?" And then in a little while he just died.'

'And you said there was nothing to tell!'

'No, there wasn't anything. He was just one of us, a labourer on the farm.'

BIOGRAPHICAL LIST OF PERSONS
FREQUENTLY MENTIONED OR CITED

LADY ELEANOR ACLAND (b. 1878) was the daughter of a prosperous paper-mill owner in Westmorland; her mother was one of the first women to become a Poor Law Guardian. She recalled her childhood in her book *Good-bye for the Present* (1935).

JOSEPH ARCH (1826–1919) of Barford, South Warwickshire, founded the National Agricultural Labourers' Union in 1872. The union achieved considerable early success before falling apart in the late 1870s; Arch went on to twice serve as an M.P. He wrote a vigorous autobiography *Joseph Arch: The Story of his Life* (1898, recently reprinted as *From Ploughtail to Parliament*), and there is a good modern biography by Pamela Horn, *Joseph Arch: The Farm Workers' Leader* (1971).

JOSEPH ASHBY (1859–1919) of Tysoe, South Warwickshire, was a labourer, lay preacher and local politician, son of ELIZABETH ASHBY (b. 1837). His life has been lovingly recreated in his daughter M.K. Ashby's classic account, *Joseph Ashby of Tysoe: A Study of English Village Life* (1961).

JOHN DEARMAN BIRCHALL (1828–97) was born in Leeds, where his family were successful Quaker merchants. In 1853 he started his own textile business, from which he retired in 1869 to live the life of a country squire at Bowden Hall, Upton St Leonard, Gloucestershire. His journals have been edited by David Verey as *The Diary of a Victorian Squire: Extracts from the Diaries and Letters of Dearman and Emily Birchall* (1983).

MARY CHOLMONDELEY (1859–1925) is best remembered as the author of the novel *Red Pottage* (1899), which gained notoriety and success for its satirical portrait of the rural clergy. Her own father was

Rector of Hodnet in Shropshire. Kept at home, like so many Victorian daughters, to look after the family, she never married. Her memoir *Under One Roof: A Family Record* (1918) is based both on her own recollections and on the contemporary diaries of her precocious, invalid sister, Hester.

LOUISA MARY CRESSWELL (fl. 1875–87) published two fascinating and argumentative books under the soubriquet 'A Lady Farmer' concerning her experiences farming 900 acres of land, with 1200 or 1300 head of stock and a large staff, on the Sandringham Estate in Norfolk, which she undertook following her early widowhood. She enjoyed a long and public wrangle with her landlord, the Prince of Wales, over the damage and loss caused by his passion for shooting.

GEORGE JAMES DEW (1846–1928) was Relieving Officer for the Bletchingdon district of the Bicester Poor Law Union from 1870-1923; his wife, Mary, was the village schoolteacher at Lower Heyford, Oxfordshire. His journals have been edited by Pamela Horn as *Oxfordshire Village Life: The Diaries of George James Dew* (1983).

J.S. FLETCHER (b. 1863), miscellaneous author, recorded his memories of life in the village of Darrington, between Ferrybridge and Doncaster, Yorkshire, in his *Memories of a Spectator* (1912).

EDWIN GREY (b. 1859) was Field Superintendent of the Rothamsted Experimental Research Station at Harpenden, Hertfordshire. He recorded his memories of growing up in Harpenden in his book *Cottage Life in a Hertfordshire Village: How the Agricultural Labourer Lived and Fared in the late '60s and '70s* (1935).

SIR HENRY RIDER HAGGARD (1856–1925), the famous novelist, was the sixth son of a Norfolk squire. He farmed over 350 acres in Ditchingham and Bedingham, Norfolk, and published his diary of *A Farmer's Year* (1899) and an important agricultural survey, *Rural England* (1902). He published an autobiography, *The Days of My Life* (1926), and his *Private Diaries* have been edited by D.S. Higgins (1980).

THOMAS HARDY (1840–1928) was born in the hamlet of Higher Bockhampton, Dorset, the son of a working mason and a cook. Both his novels and his poetry show an unmatched, intimate knowledge of the ways of rural life and thought in his native Wessex. *The Life of*

Thomas Hardy (1962, first published in two volumes, 1928 & 1930) by Florence Emily Hardy is really his autobiography.

JAMES HAWKER (1836–1921) of Oadby, Leicestershire, was a notorious poacher who nevertheless served on the local School Board. His manuscript autobiography was edited by Garth Christian as *A Victorian Poacher: James Hawker's Journal* (1961).

FRANCIS GEORGE HEATH (b. 1843) was the author of investigative works such as *The 'Romance' of Peasant Life* (1872), *The English Peasantry* (1874) and *British Rural Life and Labour* (1911).

RICHARD HEATH (fl. 1870–95) is remembered only as the author of the essays, mostly based on his own investigations on 'pedestrian tours' through the English counties, collected in his book *The English Peasant* (1893).

RICHARD JEFFERIES (1848–87) was born at Coate, near Swindon, the son of a small farmer. Of his many books on rural topics, *Hodge and his Masters* (1880) is the most coherent in its picture of all aspects of village life; *Landscape with Figures* (1983), an anthology edited by Richard Mabey, reprints much of his best work. Besides his country books, Jefferies is the author of the children's classic *Bevis* (1882) and of a spiritual autobiography, *The Story of my Heart* (1883). His *Nature Diaries and Note-Books* have been edited by S.J. Looker (1948).

AUGUSTUS JESSOPP (1823–1914) was headmaster of Norwich School from 1859 till 1879 when he retired to become rector of Scarning, Norfolk, in order to have time to pursue his antiquarian interests. His books on village life include *Arcady, for Better, for Worse* (1887) and *Trials of a Country Parson* (1890).

FRANCIS KILVERT (1840–79) was one of six children of The Rev. Robert Kilvert. Although 'Kilvert country' is the area round Clyro in Radnorshire where Kilvert was curate for the seven years 1865–72 and rector of two parishes between 1876 and his death, he spent the years 1872–76 as curate in his father's old living of Langley Burrell, Wiltshire. Three volumes of extracts from his incomparable *Diary* were edited by William Plomer (1938–40). Most of the original diary has since been destroyed, but one original notebook *The Diary of Francis Kilvert, April-June 1870* has been published in full (1982). There is a biography by Frederick Grice, *Francis Kilvert and his World* (1984).

'THE KING OF THE NORFOLK POACHERS' (b. *circa* 1860) is well described by his pseudonym. His autobiography *I Walked By Night* (1935) was coaxed out of him and edited by Lilias Rider Haggard, daughter of Sir Henry.

ISAAC MEAD (b. 1859) published his autobiography as *The Life Story of an Essex Lad* (1923), telling of his slow rise from labourer to farmer and master miller.

GEORGE FRANCIS MILLIN (fl. 1891), journalist, was a 'Special Correspondent' for the Liberal *Daily News*, contributing the essays on rural conditions collected in *Life in Our Villages* (1891).

ARTHUR JOSEPH MUNBY (1828–1910), barrister and poet, recorded his obsession with working women in a lifetime's diaries now in Trinity College, Cambridge. He was secretly married for many years to a maid-of-all-work, HANNAH CULLWICK (1833–1909), whose autobiographies and journals have been edited by Liz Stanley as *The Diaries of Hannah Cullwick* (1984). Munby's own diaries form the basis of Derek Hudson's excellent biography *Munby: Man of Two Worlds* (1972), while his marriage to Hannah has been further explored by Leonore Davidoff in her essay 'Class and Gender in Victorian England' in *The Double Vision: Sex and Class in Women's History* (1983). Munby's collection of photographs forms the basis of Michael Hiley's *Victorian Working Women: Portraits from Life* (1979). Of his poems, *Dorothy: A Country Story* (1880), makes the most direct use of his close knowledge of female farm workers.

GEOFFREY ROBINSON (b. 1917) is the author of *Hedingham Harvest* (1977) a study of Victorian family life based on the memories of his grandparents, his mother, and 'fourteen garrulous aunts and uncles'. It is a racy, gossipy book full of intimate and surprising detail. The original village of the book's 'Hedingham' is Waddingham, near Brigg, in north Lincolnshire, but I have referred to it throughout as Hedingham.

JOSEPH MILLOTT SEVERN (b. 1861) was born in the industrial village of Codnor, ten miles from Matlock. His *My Village: Owd Codnor, Derbyshire, and the Village Folk when I was a Boy* (1935) is a vivid, almost person-by-person account of the village of his childhood. He also wrote an autobiography, *The Life Story and Experiences of a Phrenologist* (1929).

HUBERT A. SIMMONS (b. 1839) was the son of a bankrupt farmer. When he was twenty-one he got a job as a farm bailiff, but soon left to join the Great Western Railway as a clerk, then station master; in later years he farmed at Caversham, Reading. His amusing, lightly fictionalised, *Ernest Struggles* (1879) has been reprinted as *Memoirs of a Station Master*; his rural novel *Stubble Farm* (1880) draws on his country childhood.

ALEXANDER SOMERVILLE (1811–85) was born in East Lothian, Scotland, the youngest of eleven sons of a carter. He started work as a cow-herd, but became a sawyer before enlisting in the Scots Greys. His flogging for insubordination, in which he received one hundred lashes, became a *cause célèbre*. As a journalist, Somerville concentrated on subjects of social reform, and particularly on the repeal of the Corn Laws, and it was for the Anti-Corn Law League that he undertook his agricultural survey, *The Whistler at the Plough* (1852). His *Autobiography of a Working Man* (1848) is well worth reading.

ANN STAIGHT (1855–92) was the daughter of a blacksmith in the village of Dumbleton in the Vale of Evesham, Gloucestershire. Her diaries – which give a valuable account of life in a middle class village household – form the basis of Susan Oldacre's biographical account, *The Blacksmith's Daughter* (1985). Ann's life ended sadly in the Gloucestershire County Asylum at Wotton, where she was admitted for 'Melancholia caused by Domestic Troubles', aggravated by Bright's Disease.

GEORGE STURT (1863–1927) was born in Farnham, Surrey, and recalls his childhood there in his memoir *A Small Boy in the Sixties* (1927). In 1884 he inherited the family business which he describes in *The Wheelwright's Shop* (1923). He kept his voluminous *Journal*, which has been edited by E.D. Mackerness (1967), on the advice of his friend Arnold Bennett, and quarried it for books such as *The Bettesworth Book* (1901) and *Memoirs of a Surrey Labourer* (1907), both of which were based on his conversations with his gardener, Frederick Grover. He used the pen-name George Bourne, taken from the village of The Bourne where he lived, and which is the subject of his *Change in the Village* (1912).

FLORA THOMPSON (1876–1947) was born at Juniper Hill, the hamlet on the Oxfordshire-Northamptonshire border which she writes about as Lark Rise. Her three-volume autobiography, *Lark Rise to Candleford* (1939, 1941, 1943) is the fullest and most authentic record we have of daily life in the late Victorian village. There is a biography, *Flora Thompson* by Gillian Lindsay (1990).

ALISON UTTLEY (1884–1976) was born at Castle Top Farm in the southern borders of the Derbyshire Peak district, and celebrated her birthplace in memoirs such as *The Country Child* (1931) and *Ambush of Young Days* (1937). She is probably best remembered today as the author of the Little Grey Rabbit children's books. Her biography, *Alison Uttley: The Life of a Country Child*, has been written by Denis Judd (1986).

'WALTER', author of the erotic autobiography *My Secret Life* (1888–94), is possibly a pseudonym for the bibliographer Henry Spencer Ashbee (1834–1900). Whoever the author, its eleven carefully-indexed volumes offer the fullest and most authoritative account of the Victorian sexual underworld, and especially of the sexual implications of class and wealth.

ALFRED OWEN WILLIAMS (1877–1930), last of the self-taught English country poets, was born in the Wiltshire village of South Marston, which he described in his *A Wiltshire Village* (1912). He wrote several further books about the villages and traditions of the Upper Thames, as well as an autobiographical account of *Life in a Railway Factory* (1915). After serving in India in the First World War he taught himself Sanskrit, and spent his last years translating *Tales from the Panchatantra* (1930). There is a biography by Leonard Clark, *Alfred Williams: His Life and Work* (1945).

FURTHER READING

Acland, Lady Eleanor
Good-bye for the Present: The Story of Two Childhoods. London:
Hodder & Stoughton, 1935

Addy, Sidney Oldall
*Household Tales, with other Traditional Remains collected in the
counties of York, Lincoln, Derby and Nottingham.* London: Nutt,
and Sheffield: Pawson & Brailsford, 1895

Anderson, M.
Family Structure in Nineteenth Century Lancashire. Cambridge:
Cambridge University Press, 1971

Arch, Joseph
Joseph Arch: The Story of his Life, Told by Himself. London:
Hutchinson, 1898

Armstrong, Alan
The Farmworkers: A Social and Economic History 1770–1980.
London: Batsford, 1988

Armstrong, H.B.J. ed
*A Norfolk Diary: Passages from the Diary of The Rev. Benjamin John
Armstrong.* London: Harrap, 1949

Ashby, M.K.
Joseph Ashby of Tysoe 1859–1919 Cambridge: Cambridge
University Press, 1961
The Changing English Village 1066–1914. Kineton: The
Roundwood Press, 1974

Atkinson, J.C.
Forty Years in a Moorland Parish. London: Macmillan, 1891

Baldry, George
  The Rabbit Skin Cap ed. Lilias Rider Haggard. London: Collins,
  1939

Barr, David
  Climbing the Ladder: the Struggles and Successes of a Village Lad.
  London: Robert Culley, 1910

Barrett, W.H. & Garrod, R.P.
  East Anglian Folklore and Other Tales. London: Routledge &
  Kegan Paul, 1976

Beckett, J.V.
  The Aristocracy in England 1660–1914. Oxford: Basil Blackwell,
  1986

Bell, Adrian
  The Open Air: An Anthology of English Country Life. London:
  Faber & Faber, 1936

Bourne, George (see also Sturt, George)
  The Bettesworth Book. London: Lamley & Co., 1901
  Memoirs of a Surrey Labourer. London: Duckworth, 1907
  Change in the Village. London: Duckworth, 1912
  A Farmer's Life. London: Jonathan Cape, 1922

Bowd, W.J.
  'The Life of a Farmworker' in The *Countryman* LI, 1955

British Parliamentary Papers (BPP, see also Census)
  *Employment of Women and Children in Agriculture: Reports of Special
  Assistant Poor Law Commissioners* 1843 (XII)
  *Royal Commission on the Employment of Children, Young Persons and
  Women in Agriculture* 1867–8 (XVII), 1868–9 (XIII), 1870 (XIII)
  Select Committee on the Game Laws 1873 (XIII)
  *Royal Commission on Labour: The Agricultural Labourer (England)
  1893–4 (XXXV)*
  Royal Commission on the Aged Poor 1895 (XIV,XV)

Briggs, K.M.
  *A Dictionary of British Folk-Tales in the English Language,
  incorporating the F.J. Norton collection.* London: Routledge &
  Kegan Paul, 1870–1

Buckmaster, J.C.
A Village Politician: The Life Story of John Buckley. London:
T. Fisher Unwin, 1897

Burnett, John
*Plenty and Want: A Social History of Diet from 1815 to the Present
Day.* London: Scolar Press, 1979; 1st ed., Thomas Nelson,
1966
A Social History of Housing, 1815–1970. Newton Abbot: David &
Charles, 1978
*Useful Toil: Autobiographies of Working People from the 1820s to the
1920s.* London: Allen Lane, 1974
*Destiny Obscure: Autobiographies of Childhood, Education and Family
from the 1820s to the 1920s.* London: Allen Lane, 1982

Burnett, J., Vincent, D. & Mayall, D.
*The Autobiography of the Working Class: An Annotated Critical
Bibliography* vol.1: 1790–1900 ; vol. 2: 1900–1945; vol. 3:
supplement 1790–1945. Brighton: Harvester, 1984, 1987, 1989

Burstow, Henry
Reminiscences of Horsham. Horsham: Free Christian Church Book
Society, 1911

Bushaway, Bob
By Rite: Custom, Ceremony and Community in England 1700–1880.
London: Junction Books, 1982

Buttery, Pauline ed.
School Diary or Log Book, Oadby Board School. Oadby,
Beauchamp College, 1979

Calvertt, John Simpson
Rain and Ruin: The Diary of an Oxfordshire Farmer ed. Celia
Miller. Gloucester: Alan Sutton, 1983

Census
1851 (BPP 1852–3 LXXXVIII, LXXXIX, XC)
1891 (BPP 1893–4 CIV, CV, CVI, CVII)

Chambers, J.D. & Mingay, G.E.
The Agricultural Revolution, 1750–1880. London: Batsford, 1966

Cholmondeley, Mary
Under One Roof: A Family Record. London: John Murray, 1918

Christian, Garth ed.
A Victorian Poacher: James Hawker's Journal. London: Oxford
University Press, 1961

Clift, William
Reminiscences. Basingstoke: Bird Bros., 1908

Cobbett, William
Rural Rides. Harmondsworth: Penguin, 1967, first pub. 1821–32

Copper, Bob
A Song for Every Season. London: Heinemann, 1971

Cresswell, Louisa Mary
Norfolk and the Squires, Clergy, Farmers, and Labourers etc..
London: Simpkin, Marshall & Co., 1875
Eighteen Years on Sandringham Estate. London: The Temple
Company, 1887

Cullwick, Hannah
The Diaries of Hannah Cullwick ed. Liz Stanley. London: Virago,
1984

Davies, M.F.
Life in an English Village. London: T. Fisher Unwin, 1909

Davies, M.L. ed.
Life as We Have Known It. London: Hogarth Press, 1931

Draper, Jo
Thomas Hardy's England ed. John Fowles. London: Jonathan
Cape, 1984

Dunbabin, J.P.D.
Rural Discontent in Nineteenth Century Britain. London: Faber &
Faber, 1974

Dyos, H.J. & Wolff, M. ed.
The Victorian City: Images and Realities. London: Routledge &
Kegan Paul, 1983

Edwards, George
From Crow-Scaring to Westminster. London: Labour Publishing
Co., 1922

Emerson, P.H.
Pictures from Life in Fen and Field. London: G. Bell, 1887

Further reading

Evans, George Ewart
Ask the Fellows who Cut the Hay. London: Faber & Faber, 1956
The Horse in the Furrow. London: Faber & Faber, 1960
The Days that We have Seen. London: Faber & Faber, 1975

Fletcher, J.S.
Memories of a Spectator. London: Eveleigh Nash, 1912

Fletcher, Ronald ed.
The Biography of a Victorian Village: Richard Cobbold's account of Wortham, Suffolk, 1860. London: Batsford, 1977

Girouard, Mark
The Victorian Country House. Oxford: The Clarendon Press, 1971

Grey, Edwin
Cottage Life in a Hertfordshire Village. St Albans: Fisher, Knight, 1935

Gróf, László L.
Children of Straw: The Story of a Vanished Craft and Industry in Bucks, Herts, Beds and Essex. Buckingham: Barracuda Books, 1988

Groves, Reg
Sharpen the Sickle! The History of the Farm Workers' Union. London: Porcupine Press, 1949

Haggard, H.R.
A Farmer's Year. London: Longman & Co., 1899
Rural England. London: Longman & Co., 1902

Haggard, L. ed.
I Walked by Night, by The King of the Norfolk Poachers. London: Nicholson & Watson, 1935

Hammond, J.L. & B.
The Village Labourer new edition ed. G.E. Mingay. London: Longman, 1978

Hardy, Thomas
'The Dorsetshire Labourer' in N. Philip ed. *Wessex Heights*. London: Bloomsbury, 1988

Harrison, Sir Edward R.
Harrison of Ightham. Oxford: Oxford University Press, 1928

149

Havinden, M.A.
  Estate Villages. A Study of the Berkshire Villages of Ardington and Lockinge. London: Lund Humphries, 1966

Heath, F.G.
  The 'Romance' of Peasant Life in the West of England. London: Cassell, Petter, and Galpin, 1872
  The English Peasantry. London: Frederick Warne, 1874

Heath, Richard
  The English Peasant. London: T. Fisher Unwin, 1893

Hobsbawm, E.J. & Rude, G.
  Captain Swing. Harmondsworth: Peregrine Books 1985

Horn, Pamela
  Joseph, Arch (1826–1919), the Farm Workers' Leader. Kineton: The Roundwood Press, 1971
  The Victorian Country Child. Kineton: The Roundwood Press, 1974
  Labouring Life in the Victorian Countryside, Dublin: Gill & Macmillan, 1976
  ed. *Oxfordshire Village Life: The Diaries of George James Dew (1846–1928), Relieving Officer.* Abingdon: Beacon Publications, 1983
  Life and Labour in Rural England 1760–1850. Basingstoke: Macmillan Education, 1987
  The Victorian and Edwardian Schoolchild. Stroud: Alan Sutton, 1989
  The Rise and Fall of the Victorian Servant. New ed., Stroud: Alan Sutton, 1990

Howkins, Alun
  Poor Labouring Men: Rural Radicalism in Norfolk 1870–1925. London: Routledge & Kegan Paul, 1985

Hudson, Derek
  Munby: Man of Two Worlds. London: John Murray, 1972

Hudson, W.H.
  Afoot in England. London: Hutchinson, 1909
  A Shepherd's Life. London: Methuen, 1910

Jefferies, Richard
  The Gamekeeper at Home. London: Smith, Elder & Co., 1878
  The Amateur Poacher. London: Smith, Elder & Co., 1879
  Hodge and his Masters. London: Smith, Elder & Co., 1880
  The Life of the Fields. London: Chatto & Windus, 1884
  The Hills and the Vale. London: Duckworth, 1909
  The Nature Diaries and Note-Books ed. S.J. Looker. London: The
    Grey Walls Press, 1948
  Landscape and Labour ed. John Pearson. Bradford-on-Avon:
    Moonraker Press, 1979
  Landscape with Figures ed. Richard Mabey. Harmondsworth:
    Penguin, 1983

Jekyll, Gertrude
  Old West Surrey. London: Longman, Green & Co., 1904

Jessopp, Augustus
  Arcady, for Better, for Worse. London: T. Fisher Unwin, 1887

Johnson, Marion
  Derbyshire Village Schools in the Nineteenth Century. New York:
    Augustus M. Kelley, 1970

Karpeles, Maud ed.
  Cecil Sharp's Collection of English Folk Songs. London: Oxford
    University Press, 1974

Kilvert, Francis
  The Diary of the Rev. Francis Kilvert ed. William Plomer. London:
    Jonathan Cape, 1938–40

Kightly, Charles
  Country Voices: Life and Lore in Farm and Village. London: Thames
    & Hudson, 1984

Kitchen, Fred
  Brother to the Ox. London: Dent, 1940

Kitteringham, Jennie
  Country Girls in Nineteenth Century England. London: History
    Workshop Pamphlets no. 11, 1973

Lloyd, A.L.
  Folk Song in England. London: Lawrence & Wishart, 1967

Longmate, Norman
The Workhouse. London: Temple Smith, 1974

Marshall, Sybil ed.
Fenland Chronicle. Cambridge: Cambridge University Press, 1967

Martin, E. W.
The Secret People: English Village Life after 1750. London: Phoenix
House, 1954
The Shearers and the Shorn. London: Routledge & Kegan Paul,
1965

Mead, Isaac
The Life Story of an Essex Lad. Chelmsford: A. Driver & Sons,
1923

Menefee, Samuel Pyeatt
Wives for Sale: An Ethnographic Study of British Popular Divorce.
Oxford: Basil Blackwell, 1981

Millin, G.F.
*Life in Our Villages, by the Special Commissioner of the 'Daily
News'*. London: Cassell, 1891

Mills, Dennis R.
Lord and Peasant in Nineteenth Century Britain. London: Croom
Helm, 1980

Mingay, G.E.
The Gentry: The Rise and Fall of a Ruling Class. London:
Longman, 1976
Rural Life in Victorian England. London: Heinemann 1976; new
edition Gloucester: Alan Sutton, 1990
The Agricultural Revolution: Changes in Agriculture 1650–1880.
London: Black, 1977.
ed. *The Victorian Countryside*. London: Routledge & Kegan Paul,
1981
The Transformation of Britain 1830–1939. London: Routledge &
Kegan Paul, 1986
ed. *The Unquiet Countryside*. London: Routledge, 1989

Mitford, Mary Russell
Our Village. London: Henry G. Bohn, 1848

Morgan, David Hoseason
Harvesters and Harvesting 1840–1900. London: Croom Helm, 1982

Newby, Howard
Country Life: A Social History of Rural England. London:
Weidenfeld & Nicolson, 1987

Northall, G.F.
English Folk-Rhymes. London: Kegan Paul, Trench, Trubner &
Co., 1892

Oldacre, Susan
The Blacksmith's Daughter: The Strange Story of Ann Staight.
Gloucester: Alan Sutton, 1985

Palmer, Roy
Everyman's Book of English Country Songs. London: Dent, 1979
The Sound of History: Songs and Social Comment. Oxford: Oxford
University Press, 1988

Peacock, A.J.
Bread or Blood. London: Gollancz, 1965

Philip, Neil ed.
*Between Earth and Sky: Poetry and Prose of English Rural Life and
Work Between the Enclosures and the Great War.* Harmondsworth:
Penguin Books, 1984

Philip. Neil
The Penguin Book of English Folktales. London: Penguin Books,
1992

Randell, Arthur
Fenland Memories. London: Routledge & Kegan Paul, 1969

Reeves, James ed.
The Idiom of the People. London: Heinemann, 1958
The Everlasting Circle. London: Heinemann, 1960

Renwick, Roger de V.
English Folk Poetry: Structure and Meaning. London: Batsford
Academic, 1980

Robinson, Geoffrey
Hedingham Harvest. London: Constable, 1977, London: Century, 1989

Rose, Walter
The Village Carpenter. Cambridge: Cambridge University Press, 1937
Good Neighbours: Some Recollections of an English Village and its People. Cambridge: Cambridge University Press, 1942

Samuel, Raphael ed.
Village Life and Labour. London: Routledge & Kegan Paul, 1975

Severn, J.M.
The Life Story and Experiences of a Phrenologist. Brighton: J.M. Severn, 1929
My Village: Owd Codnor, Derbyshire, and the Village Folk when I was a Boy. Brighton: J.M. Severn, 1935

Simmons, Hubert
Ernest Struggles. London: Simpkin & Marshall, 1879; ed. Jack Simmons as *Memoirs of a Station Master*. Bath: Adams & Dart, 1974
Stubble Farm. London: Tinsley Bros., 1880

Somerville, Alexander
The Whistler at the Plough. Manchester: James Ainsworth, 1852

Springall, L. Marion
Labouring Life in Norfolk Villages 1834–1914. London: George Allen & Unwin, 1936

Steedman, Carolyn
Policing the Victorian Community: The formation of English provincial police forces 1856–80. London: Routledge & Kegan Paul, 1984

Stevens, James
A Cornish Farmer's Diary ed. P.A.S. Pool. Penzance: P.A.S. Pool, 1977

Stubbs, C.W.
The Land and the Labourers. London: Swan Sonneschein & Co., 1885
The Church in the Villages. London: Christian Social Union, 1893

Sturt, George (see also Bourne, George)
  The Wheelwright's Shop. Cambridge: Cambridge University
  Press, 1923
  A Small Boy in the Sixties. Cambridge: Cambridge University
  Press, 1927
  Journals ed. E.D. Mackerness. Cambridge: Cambridge
  University Press, 1967

Tate, W.E.
  The English Village Community. London: Gollancz, 1967

Thompson, Denys
  Change and Tradition in Rural England. Cambridge: Cambridge
  University Press, 1980

Thompson, F.M.L.
  English Landed Society in the Nineteenth Century. London:
  Routledge & Kegan Paul, 1963

Thompson, Flora
  Lark Rise to Candleford. Oxford: Oxford University Press, 1945

Turnbull, James B.
  Reminiscences of a Stonemason, by a Working Man. London: John
  Murray, 1908

Tweedy, Arthur
  'Recollections of a Farm Worker' in the *Bulletin of the Cleveland
  and Teesside Local History Society* 21, 1973

Uttley, Alison
  The Country Child. London: Faber & Faber, 1931

Verey, David ed.
  *The Diary of a Victorian Squire: Extracts from the Diaries and Letters
  of Dearman and Emily Birchall.* Gloucester: Alan Sutton, 1983

Vincent, David
  *Bread, Knowledge and Freedom: A Study of Nineteenth-Century
  Working Class Autobiography.* London: Methuen, 1982

'Walter'
  My Secret Life ed. G. Legman. New York: Grove Press, 1966

Warren, C. Henry
Happy Countryman. London and Aylesbury: Geoffrey Bles, 1939
The Good Life: An Anthology of the Life and Work of the Countryside, in prose and poetry. London: Eyre & Spotiswoode, 1946

Williams, Alfred
A Wiltshire Village. London: Duckworth, 1912
Villages of the White Horse. London: Duckworth, 1913
Life in a Railway Factory. London: Duckworth, 1915
Round About the Upper Thames. London: Duckworth, 1922
Folk-Songs of the Upper Thames. London: Duckworth, 1923

Williams, Merryn
Thomas Hardy and Rural England. London: Macmillan, 1972

Williams, Raymond
The Country and the City. London: Chatto & Windus, 1973

Winstanley, Michael J.
The Shopkeeper's World 1830–1914. Manchester: Manchester University Press, 1983

Wohl, Anthony S. ed
The Victorian Family. London: Croom Helm, 1978

Wood, Christopher
Paradise Lost: Paintings of English Country Life and Landscape 1850–1914, London: Barrie & Jenkins, 1988

Wood, William
A Sussex Farmer. London: Jonathan Cape, 1938

INDEX